Warrior • 4

US Cavalryman
1865–90

Martin Pegler • Illustrated by C Hook, P Sarson and D Sque

First published in Great Britain in 1993 by Osprey Publishing,
Midland House, West Way, Botley, Oxford OX2 0PH, UK
443 Park Avenue South, New York, NY 10016, USA
E-mail: info@ospreypublishing.com

Transferred to digital print on demand 2008

First published 1993
3rd impression 2004

Printed and bound by Cpod, Trowbridge

A CIP catalogue record for this book is available from the British Library

ISBN: 978 1 85532 319 3

Index by Alan Thatcher

FOR A CATALOGUE OF ALL BOOKS PUBLISHED BY OSPREY MILITARY
AND AVIATION PLEASE CONTACT:

NORTH AMERICA
Osprey Direct, c/o Random House Distribution Center, 400 Hahn Road, Westminster, MD 21157
E-mail: info@ospreydirect.com

ALL OTHER REGIONS
Osprey Direct UK, P.O. Box 140 Wellingborough, Northants, NN8 2FA, UK
E-mail: info@ospreydirect.co.uk

www.ospreypublishing.com

Dedication
To my wife, Katie, without whom...

Acknowledgements
I would like to offer my thanks to all the photographic librarians who have assisted me with illustrations
and in particular to Jeremy Hall for his herculean efforts on my behalf.

INTRODUCTION

This book is not a history of the Indian Wars, or even of the Army as a whole. Rather, it is an attempt to convey to the reader the reality of campaign service of just one part of the United States Army – that of the US Cavalry.

Over the years, the US Cavalry has been glamorised and fictionalised to a point where few people appreciate where reality stops and fantasy begins; my primary aim has been to show what life was *really* like for the trooper who boiled in the Arizona sun, or froze in the winter Montana winds.

No single volume can cover every facet of such varied service life in exhaustive detail, so it is hoped that this book will serve as a basis upon which the interested reader can build. There are, I am aware, certain areas which the knowledgeable reader will find lacking – officers' clothing has been dealt with only in brief and dress uniforms could not be covered due to the limitations of space.

Those who wish to know more about the battles and the Indians will have to consult one of the many books that cover the subject and readers will find a comprehensive bibliography at the back of this book. I have tried to select books that are readily available, or, in one or two cases, of particular historical significance. To the authors of these books, I can only offer my thanks. For those wishing to visit the sites mentioned, there is a list of excellent museums which capture the flavour of the period.

Many of the photographs are of poor quality due to the early nature of the equipment used; however, they are a vital link with the past, and it is hoped the reader will make allowances for occasional lack of detail.

'A Cavalry troop go on patrol from Fort Bowie, Arizona.' Their neat appearance and universal 1872 forage caps make one wonder if the true reason for the patrol was for the camera. (National Archives)

HISTORICAL BACKGROUND

The period 1865–1890 was one of unparalleled change in American frontier history. This span of 25 years witnessed the end of the traditional nomadic lifestyle of the plains Indians, the colonisation of the West by white settlers, and the first experience of the US Army in fighting a form of irregular warfare at which it did not excel, for which its soldiers and commanders were untrained, and its equipment unsuited. The US Army, both infantry and cavalry, were strangers in a strange land. That they acquitted themselves so well in the face of bureaucratic meddling, poor supply and appalling climatic conditions, speaks highly of the tenacity and physical toughness of the volunteers who served in the West.

Until the return of Lewis and Clark from their expedition in 1806, it was generally accepted by settlers that civilisation stopped west of the Missouri river. Beyond, it was believed there was a land both inhospitable and uninhabitable. Lewis and Clark dispelled this myth, and their accounts of vast mountain ranges, forests and prairies populated by incalculable numbers of animals, did much to fuel the wanderlust of restless immigrants. By the mid-1800s the trickle of western-bound settlers had become a steady stream. The Civil War slowed their procession, but the respite was temporary. From 1865, the trickle again became a flood as war-weary men sought a new life, and this new invasion prompted an increasingly violent backlash from the Indians.

Indian conflicts were, of course, nothing new in American history, from the subjugation of the eastern natives by the first settlers, to the forced resettlement of the Five Civilised Tribes – Cherokee, Choctaw, Chickasaw, Creek and Seminole – in the 1830s. The clash of cultures was to a certain extent inevitable, and exacerbated by white greed and duplicity. In the early 19th century, there were approximately 250,000 Plains Indians living a nomadic and semi-nomadic existence in the sparsely populated West and Midwest. The West was home to many tribes, the Dakota being the largest, comprising 13 affiliated tribes generically referred to as the Sioux – these included Hunkpapa, Brulé, Oglala, Miniconjou, Sans Arcs and others who shared common language and customs. Other tribes included Nez Percé, Crow, Cheyenne, Comanche and Arapaho, and in the South-west, Navaho and Apache. Their lifestyle was by no means one of peace and tranquillity. Inter-tribal wars flared, raids, ambushes, and theft were commonplace occurrences and hunger and disease were constant companions in lean years.

Tribal life centred around the buffalo, and the importance of this animal in native culture is fundamental in understanding much of the subsequent behaviour of the Indians in their dealings with the white man. From the buffalo, and other wild game, came food, clothing, shelter and raw materials for making everything from combs to weapons. Unlimited access to the plains and its wildlife was vital if the Indian was to remain a free man. Most native culture was based around principles of group loyalty and mutual protection. The idea of property or land ownership was to cause much trouble when government officials introduced ownership treaties. This was a concept utterly alien to the Indian mind, as expressed by Tashunka Witko (Crazy Horse), 'One does not sell the earth upon which the people walk'.

Before and during the Civil War, there had been constant clashes between Plains Indians, settlers and soldiers. In 1862, the Santee Sioux launched a series of attacks in Minnesota. Army action against them served only to further inflame other Dakota tribes, who joined their Santee cousins. By 1865, Wyoming, Nebraska, Kansas, Montana and most of Colorado were suffering from regular Indian depredations. New Mexico, Texas and Arizona were also feeling the wrath of the south-western tribes, but the war in the East soaked up all available men and supplies, leaving the western garrisons starved of everything they required to wage war effectively. With the cessation of hostilities in 1865, fresh demands were made upon the President for help in defeating the rising Indian scourge, demands that could no longer be ignored as westward expansion was being actively encouraged by the Government. In practical terms it was impossible to stop, as the lure of goldfields, trapping, timber and limitless land proved irresistible to the war-weary Easterners. As Indian attacks increased on the wagon trains, miners and settlements, so did the need for military protection. To a great extent the

'Troopers watch for the enemy during the Modoc Wars 1872–3.' Two wear Civil War 'bummer' caps and four-button sack coats. The middle man has his carbine sling and cartridge pouch, the right trooper carries a Sharps carbine. (National Archives)

Major forts and towns of the Indian Wars, 1865–1890.

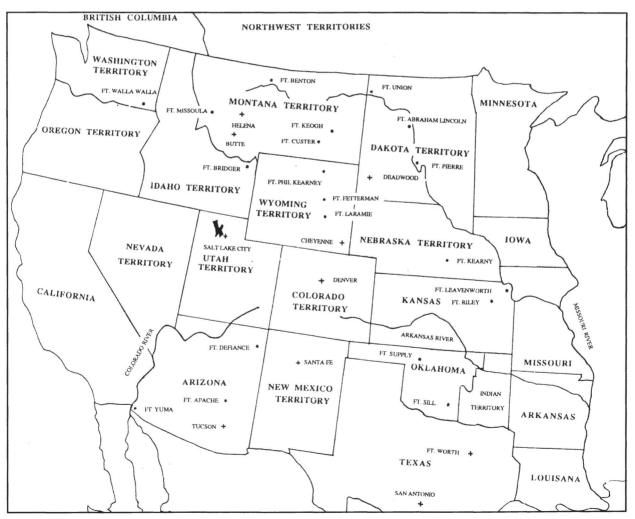

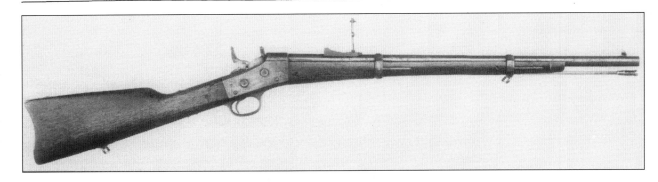

A Remington Rolling-Block carbine in .45-70 calibre. Not as glamorous as a Sharps or Winchester, but a solid, strong weapon that was well liked by those who used it. (Board of Trustees, The Royal Armouries)

Troops in the West were in an impossible situation. They were expected to prevent white encroachment onto reservation land, thus reducing tension with the Indians, whilst at the same time protecting the same whites from physical harm. Over a 25-year period this role changed from peace-keeping to pacification. It became the Army's duty to put Indians on reservations, and ensure they remained there.

There was money to be made in the West and vested interests on the part of Eastern politicians ensured that protection for the mining and lumber camps, trappers and buffalo hunters, would not be long in coming. Two cultures were on a collision course.

CHRONOLOGY

1865 The end of the American Civil War. Assassination of President Lincoln. Appointment of Andrew Johnson as President. Start of operations against the Sioux on the Little Big Horn and Powder Rivers.
The Tongue river fight (Montana).

1866 Gen. W. T. Sherman takes command of the Army in the West. The start of the Snake War.
The Fetterman Massacre (Wyoming), *The battle of Beechers Island* (Colorado), *The fight of Crazy Woman Fork* (Wyoming).

1867 *The Wagon Box fight* (Montana). *The Hayfield fight* (Montana).

1868 Gen. W. T. Sherman appointed General in

Chief. The end of the Snake War.
The battle of the Washita (Oklahoma).

1869 Appointment of Gen. Ulysses Grant as President.
The battle of Summit Springs (Colorado).

1872 Start of the Modoc War.
The fight at Salt River Canyon (Arizona).

1873 *The Lava Bed battles* (California), The end of the Modoc War.
The fight at Massacre Canyon (Nebraska).

1874 The start of Red River War
The fight at Adobe Walls (Texas).
The battles of Tule and Palo Duro Canyons (Texas).

1875 Gen. Crook appointed commander of the Army of the Platte. The end of the Red River War.

1876 The end of the Little Big Horn and Powder River campaign.
The fight of Dull Knife (Wyoming). *The battle of the Rosebud* (Montana). *The battle of Little Big Horn* (Montana).
Death of Chief Crazy Horse (5 September).

1877 Appointment of Rutherford Hayes as President. Start of the Nez Percé and Bannock/Paiute Wars.
The battle of Bear Paw Mountain (Montana). *The fight at Canyon Creek* (Montana). *The fight at the Big Hole* (Montana). *The battle of White Bird Canyon* (Idaho).

1878 *The battle of Willow Springs* (Oregon).
End of the Nez Percé and Bannock/Paiute Wars.

1879 The Ute War.
The Thornburg and Meeker massacres (Colorado).

1881 Appointment of J. A. Garfield as President,

followed by C.A. Arthur. The start of the Apache War.

1882 *battle of Horseshoe Canyon* (New Mexico). *battle of Big Dry Wash* (Arizona).

1884 Gen. Sherman succeeded by Gen. P.H. Sheridan as General in Chief.

1885 Appointment of Grover Cleveland as President.

1886 Surrender of Geronimo. End of the Apache War.

1888 Death of Gen. P.H. Sheridan.

1890 Rise of the cult of the Ghost Dance. *The battle of Wounded Knee* (South Dakota). The death of Sitting Bull (15 December). The end of the Indian Wars.

ENLISTMENT

The reasons for enlisting in the Army were almost as many and varied as the number of men who joined. There are few statistics available detailing motives for enlistment, but National Archives records show the average age of a Cavalry trooper was 23 (32 if he was re-enlisting). The background of the men does provide some clues, however. Almost 50 per cent were recent immigrants who joined the Army as a means of obtaining regular pay, an education and a grounding in the English language.

In approximate numerical order, in the ranks of the Cavalry between 1865 and 1890, could be found Irish, German/Austrian, Italian, British, Dutch, French and Swiss, plus a smattering of many other nationalities. Language difficulties were a constant problem, with English-speaking immigrants often translating orders for their compatriots. Poverty, persecution and unemployment were major factors in prompting Europeans to look to America for a new life. The Potato Famine had uprooted 1,000,000 Irishmen, so it was little wonder that the Irish provided the bulk of non-American soldiery. Indeed, of the 260 men who died at Little Big Horn with Custer, approximately 30 per cent were Irish.

Many men, both officers and other ranks, rejoined the Army as a logical continuation of their Civil War service. The long war years had left them mentally unsuited to civilian life, and re-enlistment was their only option. It was these hardened veterans of Cold Harbor, Bull Run and Antietam that provided the post-war Cavalry with the disciplined backbone and experience it needed.

For many young men, the lure of the Cavalry had nothing to do with poverty, homelessness or deprivation. It was simply a case of romanticism overcom-

An oft-used but interesting picture of the 7th Cavalry Gatling Gun left behind by Custer. The man at the left wears a four-button sack coat with added breast pocket. The NCO behind him wears a cut-down 1861 dress frock coat. The soldier right foreground has the later five-button coat, with a homemade 'prairie belt', holding .45-70 ammunition. All are wearing 1872 forage caps. Taken at Fort Lincoln, Dakota, circa 1877. (Little Bighorn Battlefield National Monument)

ing sense. Often those who joined up came from good families and had a trade or professional qualification. Sgt. Frederick Wyllyams, who post-war joined the 7th Cavalry and had served as a volunteer during the Civil War, came from a respectable and wealthy English family, and had been educated at Eton. He was to die at the hands of Sioux warriors.

In his perceptive, contemporary book, *The Story of the Soldier*, Gen. George Forsyth notes a book-keeper, farm boy, dentist, blacksmith, and 'a young man of position' trying to gain a commission, 'a salesman ruined by drink, an Ivory Carver and bowery tough' as trades once enjoyed by an escort party he was accompanying. A company of 7th Cavalry in 1877 held 'a printer, telegraph operator, doctor, two lawyers, three language professors, a harness maker, four cooks and bakers, two black-smiths, a jeweller, three school teachers, as well as farmers, labourers and railroad workers'. Although such a distinguished company was uncommon, some of these professions were well paid and respected, so want was not necessarily the prime cause for their abandonment of civilian life. The desire for a life free of routine drudgery, the chance of open air, adventure and excitement all played their part. $13 a month for privates, rising to $22 for line sergeants, was small incentive for a professional man to join the Cavalry, although it was an improvement on the $2 a week that an unskilled man could earn.

For Negroes, the Army offered more than just an escape from drudgery. It promised social acceptance, a fair wage, chances of promotion, and a sense of racial belonging that few whites could understand.

Discharge after honourable service for a black soldier gave him the chance of better employment and increased social respectability. Black troopers of the 9th and 10th Cavalry consistently proved to be smarter, more reliable and disciplined than comparative white units. Levels of desertion were minimal amongst the black troopers compared to white Cavalry units. They were led by white officers whose loyalty to their black soldiers exhibited a very high degree of commitment, especially in the face of appalling racial prejudice which often led to social ostracism from their contemporaries.

All armies contain a lawless element, and the post-Civil War Cavalry was no exception. Men on the run from family problems, the law or simply at odds with society, would enlist – often under assumed names – and find anonymity in the Army. Some, nicknamed Snowbirds, would sign on to see them through a winter, and then desert, with all their equipment, as soon as the snows melted. Desertion was one of the most serious problems faced by the Government. A report by the adjutant general in 1891 calculated that of 255,712 men who enlisted between 1867 and 1890, 88,475 deserted, a rate of about 33 per cent. In 1867 52 per cent of Custer's 7th Cavalry deserted. This was serious enough in terms of loss of government property, but even more worrying was the inability of the Army, already pared to the bone, to replace the experienced men.

On 28 July 1866, President Johnson made history by signing an Act that actually increased the size of a peacetime regular army. The Cavalry was enlarged from six to ten regiments, each comprising 12

Fort Riley, 1868. The Officers' quarters. One of the more substantial buildings. (Photo T. O'Sullivan. Courtesy J.D. Horan Collection)

companies, and two regiments (9th and 10th) were composed of black enlisted men. In addition, companies were enlarged from 64 privates to 100. This expansion did not last long in the face of mounting pressure from money-minded congressmen, and on 8 March 1869, the Cavalry were again reduced to 60 privates per company. Between 1874 and 1876 cuts removed commissary and medical staff, company NCOs and cut the number of enlisted men to 54 per company. The Army was thus reduced from 54,000 to 25,000 men.

The shock waves that the massacre of Custer and his men created, again prompted an increase in 1876 to 100 men per Cavalry company, but few were ever able to field more than 50 per cent of their strength at any one time, due to sickness, desertion and post duties. An officer of the 3rd Cavalry stated in 1876 that he had not one officer available to serve with the company on duty. This shortage was to greatly hamper the Army in the West and was indirectly to lead to some serious military reversals.

Officers, too, had their share of problems in the post-war Army. In 1866, the officer corps consisted primarily of West Point graduates and volunteer Civil War veterans, many of whom had been promoted from the ranks – about 12 per cent of the officer total. Post-war promotion and career prospects were dismal for those who stayed on in the regular Army. It would take a 2nd lieutenant about 25 years to reach the rank of major and ten years longer to make colonel.

Ageing senior officers stayed in the Army to receive their pensions, effectively blocking promotion down the line. Many officers took dramatic reduction in rank to retain a regular commission, even to the extent of re-enlisting as a private soldier, as did one ex-Confederate Cavalry major. Pay, compared to professional civilian rates, was also poor, a 2nd lieutenant in the early 1870s earning $115 a month and a colonel $300. The quality of officers varied widely, ranging from the respected and considerate to the alcoholic and reviled, and this standard was reflected to a large extent in the attitude, bearing and efficiency of the battalions and companies under their command and their behaviour in combat.

For any applicant, enlistment was a cursory affair, with a medical check-up on hearing, sight and speech, use of limbs and obvious physical defects. Newly appointed officers may be interviewed by the colonel, or simply given a billet and left to introduce themselves to their fellow officers. Enlisted men were asked to raise their right hand in an oath of allegiance, and, having sworn loyal service to the United States of America, were issued with a basic clothing allowance and despatched to recruit depots for training and eventual allocation to a serving regiment.

TRAINING

For enlisted men in the US Cavalry, the depot at Jefferson Barracks, Missouri, was their only chance to learn the intricacies of military life prior to their despatch to a serving unit. The depot was not, however, a training centre, and none were to exist until the final years of the Indian Wars. The concept of a depot was to provide the recruit with his clothing and equipment allowance, teach him the basics of drill, and keep him busy with fatigues such as guard, stable cleaning or cookhouse duties. No attempt was made to teach weapon handling, horsemanship or tactics. From the 1860s to the late 1870s, even marksmanship was not included in the training programme, and it was left to the whim of the company officers to decide on instruction in that most fundamental of military skills. In 1872, it became a requirement for each man to fire 40 rounds of rifle ammunition, although the regulation was largely ignored. At some posts, ammunition was in such short supply that any form of practice would have left the command almost unable to defend itself in the event of an attack. Lt. E. Godfrey of the 7th Cavalry recalled that his request for target practice with the regimental Gatling gun brought forth the response that he would have to pay for the ammunition himself. The crews never did fire the guns.

It was not until 1879 that a programme was introduced requiring all soldiers to fire 20 rounds per month on a proper range. Up until that date, only the enthusiasm of interested officers enabled troopers to acquire some skill in rifle shooting.

Other basic skills were denied the fledgling troopers. Marching, bivouacking and skirmishing were left to future practical experience, and riding skills were not taught until the recruit joined his regiment. This posed quite a problem as many were from the Eastern states and had no experience whatsoever of horses, and upon assignment to Cavalry regiments proved singularly inept at even mounting a horse, let alone controlling one. When a unit was about to take to the field, this was a serious matter, as shortage of manpower frequently ensured new recruits had to accompany the unit, suffering agonies of saddle soreness in the process. As one officer dryly commented, 'After a good deal of fuss and worry, I got the men mounted ... as may be supposed the sight was as good as a circus and the way several of the men were thrown was a caution.'

The depots served to initiate men swiftly into the ways of army life, teaching them how easy it was to be parted from their money by post traders, unscrupulous NCOs and saloon keepers, and the vagaries of army discipline. Most importantly, it allowed men to establish friendships that were enduring and vital if the lonely and comfortless life on the plains was to be endured. Life at the depots was for most recruits a mixture of routine and boredom, at least until the

Old Fort Hays in 1867. It was as bleak as it looks, and is an excellent example of the typical condition of most early forts. (Kansas State Historical Society)

Cavalrymen at rifle practice. Each man seems to have adopted a different method of wearing his hat. The trooper in the foreground holds a Trapdoor Springfield carbine and wears a carbine sling and webbing cartridge belt. (National Archives)

army reorganisations of the late 1880s, when proper training procedures were established, and spare time became jealously guarded in between small arms drill, physical exercises, close order marching and lectures on care and usage of weapons and equipment. Cavalry recruits at Jefferson Barracks had in addition mounted and dismounted sabre drill (even though by this date the sabre had ceased to be of any practical use in combat), equitation and target practice.

Early on in the post-war period, few recruits could expect to stay for long at a depot, as manpower was too short. Some stayed only a few days, others a few weeks, depending on the needs of their assigned regiments. Reaching those regiments was, for many, an adventure in itself. Railroad accommodation of the most basic type was used wherever possible, usually with no provision for toilets or proper food, but to the excited enlisted men, it was an adventure into the unknown. They forayed for food at every possible opportunity, shot at game, begged for hot water from the engineers, and cooked meals on the wagon floors. At the end of the line at Dakota or Wyoming, if they were lucky transferred to horse-drawn wagons, waiting to carry them still further west. If not they walked, as one draft did after leaving the railhead at

Corinne, Utah. A month later they arrived at their post in Helena, Montana, 600 miles away. Once at his post, the trooper was assigned to a company in which he would stay for his entire subsequent army career, accepting as friends or enemies, the men, NCOs and officers who comprised that company.

UNIFORM AND EQUIPMENT

The lure of the military uniform has long been a strong one for many young men, but in practical terms the uniform of the Civil War Cavalry was as unsuitable as any uniform could be for the rigours of field service. This unsuitability was compounded by the reluctance of Congress and the Army to approve any expenditure over and above what was absolutely necessary. The novice cavalryman of 1866–1872 was issued with civil war surplus uniform, familiar to any volunteer of pre-1861. At the outset, it should be stressed that the campaign cavalryman, in the years 1865–1880, bore little or no relationship to the grey-hatted, yellow-striped and neckerchiefed image of the Hollywood fantasy. In fact, considerable latitude

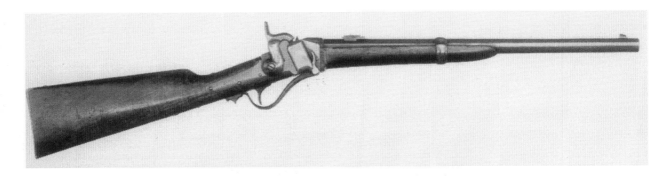

A percussion, slant-breech Sharps carbine, .52 calibre. A popular rifle with both cavalry and indians. (Board of Trustees, The Royal Armouries)

was allowed in personal clothing and equipment, mainly through sheer necessity. Issue clothing was often so poor it disintegrated, and civilian manufactured clothing was usually better made, more durable and comfortable. As Charles King, 5th Cavalry, noted, when issued with field orders, '... we had fallen back on our comfortable old Arizona scouting suits, and were attired in deerskin, buckskin, flannels and corduroy ... you could not have told officer from private'. No account was taken of the climatic conditions in which the soldier was to serve, which on the plains would vary from −40°F in winter to 120°F in summer. Regardless, the same clothing was issued.

This consisted of the sack coat, a loose collared hip-length jacket made of a coarse, dark blue, woven wool, with four brass buttons. The old style shell jacket, a waist-length, close-fitting, high-collared coat could also be found in service, and post-war was still preferred by many long-serving regulars as smarter and more military than the sack coat. A grey or blue flannel shirt was also issued, which was almost invariably replaced by more comfortable civilian patterns – some button fronted, others with three or four buttons at the neck and, particularly popular, the 'fireman's' shirt, with a buttoned flap across the chest. A set of long woollen underwear which itched furiously in hot weather was also supplied.

The issue trousers were of sky blue Kersey wool, with plain metal buttons for use with white woven cotton braces. The trousers were not up to the demands of days in contact with a saddle, and wore out at the seat and inner thighs rapidly. The usual remedy was to reinforce them with white canvas where it was available, otherwise burlap sacks or meal bags would be used. Some idea of the state of campaigning troopers can be gained from the comments of Sgt. John Ryan, whose men after a winter campaign in 1868 were '... almost destitute of clothing, our trousers being patched with seamless meal bags. A large number of the hats belonging to men were made of the same material. The legs of our cavalry boots were pretty scorched and burned from standing around camp fires and as substitutes we used leggings made from pieces of tents. A number of men had to use woollen blankets in place of overcoats.'

For privates, trousers were often issued without the distinctive $\frac{1}{8}$ in. wide yellow stripe denoting cavalry service, and up to 1872, many cavalrymen, including NCOs, could be found wearing completely plain, unpiped blue trousers. Post-1872, regulations required officers to wear a $1\frac{1}{2}$ in. stripe, sergeants 1 in. and corporals $\frac{1}{2}$ in. Such regulations were not necessarily obeyed, and often the situation continued much as before, with soldiers wearing what was available at the time.

Headgear was either a 'Hardee' or 'Jeff Davis' black felt hat with a flat crown and turned-up brim around which was a yellow branch-of-service cord, or a Civil War fatigue hat or 'bummer'; a rather shapeless version of the peaked French Army Kepi. The Kepi stayed in use for a surprising length of time considering its impracticality, as one soldier caustically commented, a clam shell would have been about as useful.

A broad-brimmed hat was by far the most practical on campaign. More than any other single item of clothing, headgear expressed the individuality of the cavalryman. Civilian hats of every colour and shape abounded, with straw hats proving particularly popular amongst both enlisted men and officers. '. . . in the field, we see no forage caps, but in their stead hats, white hats, brown hats, black hats, all kind of hats except the service hat, for that too is unsuitable.'

Footwear was always a contentious issue in the Army. During the war, the majority of cavalry troopers wore the ankle-length shoe or bootee. Their over-long trousers generally permitted the hem to rest over the shoe when mounted, although when walking the trouser bottoms would drag on the ground and looked unsightly. Boots were preferred by those who could obtain them, and in the latter years of the war, the high cavalry boot became more generally available. It was square toed, the left and right being indistinguishable, with either a small cuban or flat leather heel, of sewn or pegged construction, with the back $15\frac{1}{2}$ ins. high, ending just at the top of the calf, whilst the front was 4 ins. higher, arching up to cover the knee when the wearer was in the saddle. There was a preference on the part of the quartermaster general to order sewn boots, as wartime boots which were pegged (the uppers held to the soles by brass screws) had proved deficient in service. The black calfskin or grain leather uppers on the Cavalry boot were thin by modern standards, and as issued the government footwear was not renowned for its longevity. The uppers parted from the soles, the heels were easily ripped off and if much walking was required, the soles could wear through in a month. Cpl. Reed, 4th Mounted Infantry, stated that after a forced march in the autumn of 1867, he and his men '. . . staggered into Fort Laramie, that is, what was left of us, our feet wrapped in our torn blankets, as our shoes were gone'.

Many methods were adopted to break in new boots including soaking them, and then drying them on the feet, or coating feet and socks with soap, both of which achieved satisfactory results. Others bought custom-made boots. Cpl. Jacob Horner, 7th Cavalry, purchased a pair of beautiful handmade boots from his company captain, noting, 'almost every soldier in the post borrowed my boots and was photographed wearing them'.

With the boot, a brass-bodied rowel spur was routinely worn, although some enlisted men and officers purchased fancy spurs often made of Mexican silver with eagle heads and other ornate designs.

Officers' uniforms

The situation for officers was less dire where clothing was concerned. Most had their uniforms modified to fit by regimental tailors, or simply purchased better quality items from civilian suppliers. Some, and Col. George Custer was a splendid example, designed uniforms to their own taste, and had them made to order. There was virtually no item of uniform that could not be privately purchased, and on campaign most officers were as unmilitary a spectacle as their men. Gen. Crook was renowned for his campaign dress of either a straw hat or pith helmet, cotton jacket over a civilian shirt, and breeches tucked into riding boots. Many learned quickly about the practicalities of adopting Indian dress, and probably more than any other article of clothing, buckskin became almost obligatory on the plains. Buckskin jackets, trousers and leggings were almost indestructible, and in wet weather the fringes permitted the sodden leather to drain quickly, as each fringe became a soakaway. Headgear was as varied as that of the enlisted men, with straw boaters being particularly popular, and boots, such as those bought by Cpl. Horner from his captain, were usually civilian-made. More latitude was permitted with regards to officers' footwear: many sported knee-high boots with turned-over tops, whilst others preferred boots which came to just below the knee. Canvas and buckskin leggings would also be worn where circumstances required.

Leather accoutrements in their basic form changed little over the Indian Wars period, and much that was wartime issue continued to be in use until the

An issue Cavalry belt buckle, in brass with silver wreath. This specimen was found on the Rosebud battlefield in 1896. (Author's collection)

A troop of the 6th Cavalry waiting to hit the trail, Arizona, 1880. (National Archives)

Army reforms of the late 1880s. The standard issue, early sabre belt comprised a black or buff leather belt, between $1\frac{1}{2}$ ins. and 2 ins. wide, with the old oval dragoon 'US' belt plate in brass, or more commonly the 1851 regulation rectangular plate with a silver wreath of laurel leaves encircling the Arms of the United States, comprising an eagle, shield and scroll with the motto *E Pluribus Unum*. There were two leather suspension straps for the sabre, and a single shoulder strap. Elsewhere on the belt would be hung a leather holster closed with a flap, cap box containing percussion caps, pistol cartridge pouch, and carbine cartridge pouch. The carbine was hung on a broad, black leather sling carried over the left shoulder, and when mounted, the muzzle of the gun would be inserted in a round leather socket to the rear of the right leg. As with all of the equipment in use in this period, there was a bewildering number of types and variations. The model 1855 cap pouch, 1855 Infantry cartridge box, model 1861 pistol cartridge pouch, 1874 Dyer pouch and pattern 1872 Infantry cartridge boxes all gradually found their way into service, along with many home-produced items. Possibly the most important modification was the adoption of the looped 'Prairie Belt', possibly first introduced in 1866 by Capt. Anson Mills. It was an issue, or civilian made, leather belt with hand-stitched leather loops on it to contain cartridges. It was both comfortable to wear, as the weight was more evenly distributed, and practical, as it could contain far more cartridges than

a pouch. In 1867, Col. Hazen introduced a removable looped pouch which found some favour.

Most cavalrymen used some form of gloves when on campaign, usually a short gauntlet style, made of buckskin, tanned leather or in exceptionally cold weather, muskrat, beaver or sealskin. The requirements of ill-equipped troopers in the deadly Western winters was a considerable problem. No allowance was made by the clothing bureau for the seasons apart from the provision of a caped sky-blue greatcoat, until the uniform changes of 1872, so most field soldiers and officers who endured winter conditions utilised what was readily to hand, and adopted buffalo-skin coats, trousers and overshoes (these were usually liberally stuffed with straw). Buffalo or beaverskin hats with earflaps protected the head while fur mitts gave the hands some protection. Their appearance must certainly have been bizarre, as Alice Baldwin, wife of a Cavalry officer stationed in Dakota, recounted. 'Clad in Buffalo skins, trousers and overcoat with the fur inside, mufflers over his ears, hands encased in fur mittens, his face in a mask leaving space sufficient only to see his way, he presents an appearance rivalling his Eskimo brother.'

It is curious to note that whilst in contemporary literature cavalrymen appeared to accept the heat as an inevitable part of campaign life, the cold was regarded by most troopers with the utmost fear. As they were often lacking suitable clothing, sudden storms could quickly kill or maim. In an article written many years later on his experiences, Gen. E. J. McClemand recalled such a snowstorm in Montana, reducing troopers to such a state that 'they wept and begged to be permitted to lie down and die

... for a time it looked as though all discipline would be lost'.

In 1872, the War Department made some attempt to improve the type and quality of clothing issued. These changes were made not so much out of a desire to improve the lot of the soldier, but as sheer necessity brought about by shortage of the popular sizes of Civil War surplus uniform. Many contractors had maximised profits during the war by producing drastically undersized uniforms, which when issued proved too small to fit even the most diminutive trooper. Nevertheless, wartime manufactured clothing was still being issued as late as 1880. It was appreciated by all that the old uniform was ill fitting, unsoldierly and in many instances impractical. The 'Bummer' cap was redesigned to be neater, and a black felt campaign hat was introduced. It was very broad brimmed with an indented crown, with the novel facility of being able to hook up the brim so that it resembled a Napoleonic cocked hat. Col. D.S. Stanley called it 'the most useless uncouth rag ever put on a man's head'. In wet weather it drooped hopelessly and lost all shape, and fell apart in a few weeks on campaign. A similar pattern was introduced in 1875 but was little better, and it was not until the introduction of the tan-coloured 1885 campaign hat that some semblance of practical headgear began to appear.

If the cavalryman had cause to grumble over the quality of uniforms issued to him prior to 1872, his mood was hardly lightened by the appearance of the 1872 pleated fatigue blouse. This ill-conceived jacket had nine buttons, and four wide pleats each side. It soon lost its creases, the seams attracted vermin on campaign and the cavalrymen hated it. It was withdrawn in 1874 and replaced by a five-button sack coat of similar type to the Civil War issue, but with yellow collar piping and a more shaped cut. The style lasted through to the end of the Indian Wars, being slightly modified in 1883 with the omission of the branch-of-service piping. Slight alterations were made to the trousers, not the least important being the order that all mounted troops should have reinforced seats!

There were many other minor changes in accoutrements. The sabre belt was provided with adjustable brass sliders for sabre straps, instead of the old fixed 'D' rings, and the straps themselves were no longer stud fastened to the sliders, but had brass hooks, making it easier to hang the sabre from the saddle mounts. The holster was modified, with the size of the top flap reduced and the body of the holster less shaped. In 1876 the Ordnance Department began manufacturing 'prairie belts' with canvas loops stitched onto a leather backing. These were an

Soldiers and Apache scouts during the war against Geronimo. Note all three standing troopers carry pistols in open civilian style holsters. Fumbling to open a flap holster could mean the difference between life and death. (Arizona Historical Society)

A group of 10th Cavalry troopers escorting Gen. Merritt. St. Mary's, Montana, 1894. All visible revolvers are carried in unbuttoned holsters. Note the difference in quality of uniform between the sergeant (second from right) and the young trooper standing next to the table. (Montana Historical Society)

improvement over the cartridge boxes, but it wasn't until 1881 that the Mills webbing cartridge belt was adopted.

The horse

Often ignored, and frequently abused, it was the horse that provided the vital motive force for both sides during the wars of 1865–90. Indian mastery of their animals was legendary. Trained in warfare and horsemanship from boyhood, warriors were at one with their mounts. The Indian pony was a hardier breed than the Government animals, with greater stamina, as Albert Barnitz noted in his diary in June 1867, '[The Indians] were usually mounted on ponies . . . the ponies were, however, of remarkable size, and very fleet and powerful. Our own horses were generally no match for them, either in speed or endurance.' However, the Indians' grass-fed animals were incapable of sustained winter use, which did not hamper the US animals, provided supplies of grain were available. The Indian practice of riding bareback, or with a thin wooden and blanket saddle, was, however, not one that caught on in the US Army!

From 1858 to the end of the wars, the McClellan saddle was used in a number of modified forms. It comprised a wooden base, or tree, with a long oval cut-out running almost the entire length to permit passage of air, and prevent sweating and chaffing. It had a raked cantle low pommel, and had its edges and strap slots covered with brass. Initially the saddle was plain rawhide covered, with leather side skirts, but this was prone to shrinkage and splitting in the rain and sun of the prairie, and quickly rendered the saddle useless. Subsequent to trials in 1870, saddles were produced covered in undyed or black leather. In 1874 it was recommended that all saddles be covered in black leather. The McClellan equipment had its faults. The curb bit, bridle, halter and link were complex, whilst the stirrups, covered by distinctive leather hoods, required considerable improvement. Designed to protect the rider from cold and thick brush, they tended to trap the foot, whilst enabling rust to form on the stirrup platform leading to subsequent disintegration of the whole stirrup. Worse still was the lack of breast strap to prevent the saddle from sliding backwards, particularly when ascending hills, when the blanket could work out from underneath the saddle. Generally, two years was the maximum service life of the McClellan.

The Army Board of July 1879 recommended that a cavalryman carry the following: one saddle tree, leather covered, two stirrup straps, five coat straps, one head-stall, one pair of reins, one felt saddle cloth,

one surcingle, one side line, one lariat, one horse brush, one carbine loop, one carbine socket and strap, one hair girth, one bit, one curb and strap, one blanket, one link, one nosebag, one picket pin, one curry comb. In addition to this, troopers stowed personal effects and mess gear – skillet, eating utensils, spare socks and shirt – in leather saddlebags carried behind the saddle. His blanket was carried rolled on the front of his saddle; greatcoat and, in hot weather, his tunic, at the rear. The round, felt-covered tin canteen was hung over the saddle pommel with the vital tin coffee cup firmly attached to any handy strap.

The mounting rings for the sabre enabled it to be suspended from the left side of the saddle. The scabbard curved back under the rider's leg, leaving the grip of the sabre within easy reach of the right hand. The lariat was usually tied to the saddle on the same side, acting as a cushion between the sword and horse. A nosebag was hung from a ring on the front right of the saddle, close to the pommel, so that it rested slightly forward of the rider's right knee. Adding the weight of a trooper, each horse was carrying around 250 lbs, and, thus equipped, the cavalryman was ready for the field.

WEAPONS

If the Cavalry trooper was inferior to the Indian in horsemanship and natural fighting ability, he was certainly superior in respect of his firepower.

In 1870 there was still a complete lack of standardisation in weaponry carried by Cavalry regiments. Approximately 25 per cent of units were equipped with the Sharps carbine, the rest had a mixture of Spencers, Springfields, Remington rolling-blocks, plus a smattering of other rifles such as Burnsides or Henry's. Pistols comprised a mixture of Colt Army & Navy and Remington Army revolvers. The only universally issued weapon was the pattern 1860 Cavalry sabre. It was a situation that demanded some regularisation if supply was not to degenerate into total confusion.

There was little doubt in the minds of soldiers who had combat experience that the muzzle loading rifle musket had been superseded by the metallic cartridge rifle. The issue of the Spencer, a seven-shot, magazine-fed rifle, had transformed the battlefield, although it was a transformation that went largely unnoticed. A man no longer had to expose himself to enemy fire whilst he stood up to reload a musket – a cartridge weapon could be loaded and fired from the prone position. In the case of the Spencer, its repeating fire capability meant that its users, provided with suitable cover and a good ammunition

The .44 calibre Colt Army percussion revolver. This early fluted cylinder model dates from 1860. (Board of Trustees, The Royal Armouries)

supply, were almost unassailable. The 7th Cavalry had shown this in 1868 during the Battle of the Washita, when a vastly superior Indian force were driven back by the unrelenting fire of the regiment's Spencers.

The rimfire .52 calibre Spencer had its shortcomings. The cartridge was underpowered, a constant problem with rimfires, and its effective range was about 300 yards, although it was capable in the hands of a good shot, of killing at far greater distances. If the carbine was dropped, the cartridges in the tubular magazine, housed in the butt, were prone to self-detonation. The Blakeslee cartridge box, containing ten magazine tubes, gave a trooper 70 rounds of ammunition, which could be fired accurately at a rate of ten rounds per minute, about five times the rate of fire of a musket. Only a few units were equipped with the Blakeslee box though, and the rest carried their cartridges in a pouch, their copper casing vulnerable to damage, making them difficult to load, and sometimes impossible to extract. For that reason a lot of troopers preferred the slower reliability of the .52 calibre percussion Sharps, as is well illustrated by Maj. C. Hardin, '... a certain troop, 1st Cavalry, armed with Spencers, went into action with a bad lot of rimfire cartridges. Several men of that troop told me that the failure of so many cartridges almost caused a panic, and would have caused a panic had it not been for the fact that other troops with them had Sharps carbines that never missed fire.'

By the early 1870s, the Sharps was already a venerable veteran of the frontier, the falling block

action having been introduced in 1859. Originally using a .52 calibre linen cartridge, it was a strong, reliable weapon with a rate of fire about half that of the Spencer, and its ability to take abuse made it popular with the troops who used it. In 1870, at the suggestion of the Board of Ordnance, remaining stocks of Sharps rifles were converted to use the .50-70 Springfield centrefire cartridge. (.50 in. calibre, using 70 grains of black powder. Carbines used a reduced charge of 45 grains and a lighter bullet.) This modification eliminated two of the major weaknesses of the old linen cartridge, flash from the gap between the block and chamber, caused by loose powder and escaping gas, and fouling of the chamber by powder residue after several rounds had been discharged.

A quantity of muzzle-loading Springfield rifles and carbines had been converted by means of the Allin system into breech loaders, using the .50-70 centrefire cartridge. The Army were not happy with the performance of the .50-70 cartridge and the lack of standardisation, so in late 1872, a board was convened in New York to look into adopting a breech-loading system. A number of weapons were tested – Spencer, Sharps, Remington, Springfield, Winchester, as well as the British Snider, and Callisher and Terry carbines. The eventual winner was the Allin Springfield, with the recommendation of a reduction in calibre to .45 in., and for carbine use a reduction in charge from 70 to 55 grains.

For the cavalrymen using the rifle, this was of considerable importance, for the recoil was punishing enough with the reduced charge, as shown by the comments of 7th Cavalryman, C.H. Allen. When target shooting, the men 'had sockets to put over the butts of the carbine and on top of that we were glad to put paper or anything we could get to keep it from the shoulder. I was black and blue all over the shoulder and down into my chest.' For a joke, a man might substitute a full .45-70 rifle cartridge in place of the .45-55. One trooper recalled that firing it from a carbine '... you thought the sky fell in'.

With small modifications, the Model 1873 Springfield usually referred to as the 'Trap-Door' – remained in Cavalry service until the adoption of the Krag Jorgensen bolt-action rifle in the 1890s. Most officers chose to carry a sporting rifle version of the Springfield (often engraved and with target sights), since the ammunition was easy to obtain and the performance of the rifle acceptable. It had a flatter trajectory and a greater effective range than the .50-70, though it was arguably more accurate than the men who fired it, as the standard of marksmanship was generally very poor among both officers and enlisted men.

Pistols

Of increasing popularity was the pistol, which had become a necessity for the cavalryman during the Civil War. At the close quarters that most Cavalry engagements were fought the revolver could outreach the sabre and outgun carbines, which required reloading after each shot, and in desperate straits the butt of a pistol made a handy club. Up to 1873, a number of revolvers were used in the Cavalry. The most solidly constructed was the Remington New Model .44, a solid framed six-shot percussion model, which could take a lot of misuse and clumsy handling without breaking. One of the drawbacks of the early Remingtons was the ease with which the axis pin (which retained the cylinder in the pistol) could be lost, instantly rendering the gun useless. Later models were modified to prevent this and the Remington was widely used in the West. Used in even greater numbers were Colt's Army and Navy revolvers in .44 and .36 calibre respectively. Of open-topped construction, they were reliable in service but very prone to frame damage because of the lack of a strengthening bar over the cylinder. If used as a club, the barrel could end up an inch out of true. The Colts saw much service in the Civil War and post-war cavalrymen carried them out of sentimental value as much as anything. Other revolvers abounded and Le Mat, Starr and multi-barrelled pepperbox pistols were also used. One disadvantage of the percussion pistols was their need to be kept dry to prevent powder and caps from becoming waterlogged. They were also prone to multiple ignition as the flash from one chamber ignited all the others, as was clearly demonstrated by the experience of Chaplain White, 2nd Cavalry, who had been caught in an ambush by Sioux Indians in July 1866. Armed with a huge, seven-barrelled English pepperbox pistol, he fired as several Indians leaped into the ravine he was sheltering in. All seven charges ignited simultaneously, killing one Indian and frightening the others so much that they fled. The experience presumably did little to soothe the Chaplain's nerves.

Clearly, some rationalisation was required, especially as the advent of more reliable metallic cartridges meant that rimfire and particularly centrefire revolvers were becoming more practical. A number of weapons were examined by the Board of Ordnance through 1871–72, Smith and Wesson, Remington, Colt, Webley and Tranter revolvers were tested. Probably for the sake of mechanical simplicity, the Board favoured single rather than double-action, and the selection was the .45 calibre Model 1872 Colt. Some percussion Colts had been converted under the Richards patent to use rimfire cartridges and it was clear that the future lay with cartridge, not percussion weapons. Prior to the adoption of the metallic cartridge, the fragile paper-wrapped cartridges for use in the percussion pistols were carried loose in pouches. The constant vibration of riding caused rapid disintegration of the paper and wise troopers carried a flask of black powder, or spare, loaded, revolver cylinders. Capt. F. Benteen, 'H' Co. 7th Cavalry, commented in a report on ordnance on 12 March 1874 that 'In my opinion, the purchase of ammunition for pistols used by the Cavalry should be

Troopers of Crooks' expedition of 1876 butcher a horse. (Denver Public Library)

confined wholly to metallic cartridges, all paper cartridges being wasted by being jolted to pieces in the pouch'.

Colt had produced an open-topped .44 calibre rimfire revolver in 1872, which resembled the early percussion Army revolver, but its modification to a solid framed .45 calibre centrefire pistol in 1873 was sufficient to sway the Board of Ordnance. An order for 8,000 Model 1873 Army revolvers with $7\frac{1}{2}$ in. barrels was placed in late 1873, and supplies began to trickle into service early the following year. The use of metallic cartridges created a new set of problems for the cavalryman, aside from the usual problem of distortion in the pouch. The increasingly frequent use of prairie belts of looped leather in the humidity of the Western plains created verdigris which, if not removed before a cartridge was fired, could turn into a solid cement with the heat of discharge, rendering ejection impossible. Surviving weapons examined after the Custer débâcle, showed evidence of jammed cases, their bases having been ripped off by the ejector mechanism. Additionally, it should be remembered that black powder fouling could exacerbate the problem, especially in very dusty conditions. The problem was partially alleviated in 1881 with the adoption of the webbing cartridge belt, but was never entirely resolved.

The single-action Colt became the most instantly recognisable revolver in the world, mainly because of the enthusiasm of Hollywood film producers for representing it as the only pistol ever carried by the US Cavalry. This, of course, was not so; although 37,000 were issued to the Army between 1873 and 1891, other revolvers were also supplied. The top-break .44 in. Smith and Wesson 1869 and .45 in. Schofield Smith and Wesson of 1875 were issued to Cavalry and infantry units, as well as a limited number of Model 1875 Remington Army revolvers. Cavalrymen liked the hard-hitting and accurate revolvers, which in a tight situation were often the difference between life and death, as Albert Barnitz recounts. Having shot two braves at close quarters with his pistol, he was faced with a warrior on foot armed with a large-bore Lancaster rifle. The Indian dodged from one side of Barnitz's horse to the other eventually jumping out and firing at near point-blank range at the same instant as Barnitz who said 'Mine [bullet] I believe must have passed through his heart as he threw his hands up frantically and ... died almost immediately'.

Knives

A vital, though unofficial piece of equipment for every cavalryman was his knife. They varied hugely in type and pattern, though the most popular were the 'Bowie' style with a single-edged, clipped point blade and grips that varied from plain wood to silver-mounted ivory. A large number of Sheffield-made

A bivouac for men on Crooks' 'starvation march'. No proper tents were issued so blankets over a frame of saplings had to suffice. (Denver Public Library)

Gen. Crook in campaign dress, with two Apache scouts, 1881. He preferred to carry a short-barrelled shotgun to the issue Springfield. (Arizona Historical Society Library)

knives were imported and proved very durable. Some cavalrymen carried their knives in plain leather scabbards, but a lot of men liked the decorated, fringed buckskin sheaths worn by the Indians, and many photographs show them prominently displayed on the sabre belt. The knives were used for skinning and butchering game, opening tins, and occasionally taking scalps. During the desperate defence of their ridge, 7th Cavalrymen under Capt. Benteen used their knives to dig shallow rifle pits to give greater protection from hostile fire. It was not until 1880 that the Army acknowledged the need for a serviceable knife and introduced a Springfield-manufactured double-edged hunting knife, with an $8\frac{1}{2}$ in. blade, brass mounts and rounded wooden handle.

Some cavalrymen provided weapons at their own expense. Private Tuttle of the 7th Cavalry, an excellent shot, used a sporting Springfield rifle to kill Sioux warriors at ranges beyond that of the carbine. Most troopers admired the repeating Winchester rifle, which had been in existence since 1865, when it was made as a rimfire and sold as the Henry. However, the Army's dislike of multi-shot rifles meant that the troops were often faced with Indians using Winchesters or Spencers whilst they were armed only with the single-shot Springfield. A considerable amount of literature has been devoted to the subject of Indian firearms. Generally, they were

not as well armed as the troopers, and many of their weapons were in a poor mechanical state. The Indians also had difficulty in obtaining the right ammunition and frequently used incorrect and incompatible cartridges.

The sabre

The most instantly recognisable symbol of the cavalryman was the sabre. It was this weapon that led to the Indian describing troopers as 'long knives' and in close combat it could prove a formidable weapon. Lt. Grummond, 2nd Cavalry, had cause to use his sabre in earnest when ambushed in the Peno Valley, Wyoming, in December 1866. Pursued by Indians intent on pulling the soldiers from their mounts, Grummond '... abandoned the use of spurs and jammed his sword into the weary beast to urge him to greater effort, followed by a Chief in full war dress with spear at his back so near that but for his good horse he would then and there met a terrible fate'. Grummond recounted that 'he shut his eyes and literally slashed his way out, as did many of the others, recalling that he heard his sabre click every time he cleaved an Indian's skull'.

A year later, Capt. A. Barnitz, 7th Cavalry, quoted another instance of its use during an action near Fort Wallace on 26 June 1867. 'A Chief mounted on a white horse ... was killed by Cpl. Harris, who

An officer and scouts during the Apache wars. The white scout wears buckskins and carries a Winchester, whilst one Apache has adopted a spiked dress helmet! The officer wears a regulation jacket, civilian slouch hat, buckskin trousers and boots. (Arizona Historical Society Library)

first engaged him with a sabre as he was attempting to plunge a lance through Private Hardiman (whose carbine was empty and whose sabre had unfortunately become disengaged from the scabbard in the pursuit and been lost).' Such accounts exaggerate the use of the sabre, however, as most troopers would prefer to place their trust in a firearm, and keep as much distance as possible between themselves and the Indians, whose prowess with club, lance and bow was exceptional.

The Model 1860 Light Cavalry Sabre was a lighter and less unwieldly version of the heavy Cavalry sabre of 1840, which had been modelled on the French 1822 pattern sabre. The Model 1840 was dubbed 'Old Wristbreaker' and demanded considerable strength and expertise to wield. The Model 1860 was of very similar appearance, but of lighter construction and less blade-heavy. It weighed 3 lbs 7 oz and measured $41\frac{1}{2}$ ins. overall with a $34\frac{5}{8}$ in. curved single-edged blade, wire-wrapped grip and three-bar, brass guard. Some officers elected to carry the standard Model 1860, but most chose an officer's pattern, which was of similar appearance, having a gilded brass hilt with decorative oakleaves. The steel scabbard was blued, as opposed to the browned ones of the enlisted men.

Times had changed on the plains since the introduction of the 1840 sabre. Indians had ceased to do battle armed only with lances, bows and tomahawks. By the end of the war, a large proportion of warriors (possibly as many as 80 per cent) had some

form of firearm, ranging from early flintlock pistols to the latest Winchesters and Sharps rifles. Close combat of the type described by Barnitz became less frequent as the years passed. The sabre was cumbersome and noisy to carry, and was rarely sharp enough to cut a cooked piece of meat, let alone hack through a buffalo hide shield. Indeed, the sabres were issued blunt, and few armourers possessed any means of sharpening them. Sabre practice was almost unknown until the end of the 1870s, by which time it had been well and truly eclipsed by the firearm. On campaign most commanders ordered the swords to be packed and left behind, and from 1870 onwards, it became rare to see a cavalry regiment in the field wearing them. Prior to the Little Big Horn, Custer ordered all sabres to be put into store, and the 7th went into action with only one sabre worn by an officer, Lt. De Rudio, who never unsheathed it during the combat. Despite claims after the battle that Custer and his men would have survived had they carried swords, there is no evidence to support the fact. A sabre is no use in the face of firearms and arrows. The Indians regarded captured sabres as prized trophies, and appeared to use them in combat with considerable enthusiasm.

Nevertheless, despite heated debate, the sabre remained in service in one form or another until the end of the First World War. Not until 18 April 1934 was an order published declaring 'the sabre is hereby discontinued as an item of issue to the Cavalry. The sabre is completely discarded as a cavalry weapon.'

FIELD SERVICE

Arrival at a remote post was usually something of a shock for the new cavalryman. After long cramped train journeys, the troopers would transfer to wagons, or march to their ultimate destination. Some were able to travel by river steamer, but all were tired, dirty and hungry upon their arrival. For the earliest reinforcements, after the cessation of hostilities in 1865, there were no forts to welcome them. Fort Reno on the Powder River in Montana, Fort Phil Kearney in Dakota territory in Wyoming and a string of other isolated outposts were built by the soldiers who were to garrison them. Most early Western forts were of earth, sod and wood construction, with adobe or brick additions as time and availability permitted. They provided the most basic protection, but were home to numerous insects. They leaked in the wet and froze in winter, and lumps of earth constantly dropped upon the inmates. At their most basic, they comprised an officers' quarters, barracks, guard room, sick bay, and workshop protected by a wooden stockade with one or more guard towers. By the 1880s, the permanent forts had blossomed into solidly constructed sites often occupying several acres, and numbering such amenities as canteens, reading rooms, chapel, married quarters, hospital and workshops. The beaten earth floors gave way to timber, and barracks were equipped with wooden arms racks, steel framed beds, clothing and personal effects lockers and iron stoves. It was at least better than their accommodation in the field. Cavalrymen travelled light, carrying only a rubberised poncho or extra blanket to act as makeshift tents. Charles King recalled their misery in a torrential downpour, 'We built "wickyups" of saplings and elastic twigs, threw ponchos and blankets over them and crawled under, but 'twas no use, the whole country was flooded ... and we huddled round them in the squashy mud.'

Fatigue duties were a common curse for all soldiers, and none more so than for the men in outlying garrisons in the middle of hostile territory. Many forts were sited to maximise the ease with which they could be defended with amenities coming second to military necessity. Water, wood and hay-cutting parties were sent out only under armed guard. Even so, they were tempting targets for lightning attacks by hostile bands, and some of the subsequent pitched battles achieved almost legendary status, such as the Hayfield and Wagon Box fights near Forts C.F. Smith and Phil Kearney on 1 and 2 August 1867, when large parties of Sioux and Cheyennes, under Chief Red Cloud, tried and failed to overrun working parties. Other fatigue parties were not so lucky, and search parties often stumbled across their bodies, as a trooper from the 2nd Cavalry recorded. When looking for water near Crazy Woman Creek in Wyoming, they found the dead body of a white man, scalped and mutilated. Remains of a grey shirt still on the shoulders indicated he had probably been a soldier. 'The finding of the dead body ... had a very depressing effect on the entire command.'

Adjusting to their new circumstances was not easy for the cavalrymen. There was no relief from the routine of post life unless the regiment embarked on a campaign, and there was nowhere to go when off duty, the nearest towns often being two or three days' journey away. At new forts, soldiers would be constantly working as labourers, giving rise to the posts being nicknamed 'Government Workhouses'. For recreation, men particularly enjoyed sports, which could include such delights as baseball, horse racing, greased pig wrestling, a greased pole climb, sack, wheelbarrow, and three-legged races as well as more traditional foot races and tug-of-war. Winners could receive useful cash prizes and competition was intense; the exercise relieved tension and promoted team spirit.

When available, alcohol was a favourite means of relaxation and was the cause of more disciplinary trouble than any other single factor. Weak beer was usually available, but no liquor could be purchased at posts in reservation land, so substitutes were concocted by desperate soldiers. Some were poisonous, such as grain alcohol and Jamaica Ginger, and could cause blindness, spasms and death. In the south-west, a popular drink was Mescal, a cactus alcohol. One cavalryman who drank it recounted he had to be tied up for two days afterwards and never drank again in his life. Most alcohol was purchased from passing traders or sutlers, civilian traders permitted to sell goods at Army posts. In the late 1870s, these had to be licensed by the War Department, but it did little to lower the prices or improve the quality of goods on offer, and most soldiers developed a strong dislike of the sutlers. It was not until 1889 that officially run canteens supplanted the post traders.

Pay day usually resulted in a mass exodus to the nearest post trader or town, if one was close by. Soldiers blew their wages on food, paid off gambling debts, the post laundress and traders, then indulged in a drinking spree that lasted until either the money ran out or the troopers' legs gave out. One man, broke but thirsty, made such a nuisance of himself in the local saloon that in desperation the barkeeper handed him a large full tumbler of whiskey, with the order 'Drink that then get out'. The soldier eyed the glass for a minute, then wordlessly drained it in one go. His friends reported that he woke up 24 hours later apparently none the worse for his excesses.

Those who could afford it would visit the local brothels to indulge in sexual gratification, with the only women accessible to sex-starved troopers. Few were able to form permanent relationships whilst on frontier postings, although occasional marriages did occur between soldiers and female staff at permanent forts – the laundresses or cooks. Some men brought their sweethearts over from the East, but only the strong-willed stayed. For the men who did not avail themselves of the prostitutes, there remained only tantalising glimpses of homesteaders' and officers' wives, and many deserted as a result of this enforced bachelorhood.

Fights were common, and some were serious, resulting in severe disciplinary measures. Other sore-

A classic portrait of Pvt. William E. Riley, US Cavalry, dated around 1886. He wears the 1883 issue slouch hat, 1884 five-button coat and 1884 gauntlets, dark blue flannel shirt, reinforced Cavalry trousers and high boots. His 1885 web belt holds .45-70 carbine ammunition and the holster holds an 1873 Single-Action Colt. (National Archives)

Model 1873 Single-Action Colt in .45 calibre. Probably the most recognisable revolver in the world, the Colt boasts the longest production run of any pistol. This specimen has had its original wood grips replaced by later hard rubber ones. (Board of Trustees, The Royal Armouries)

headed men were fined, given extra fatigues, or if NCOs, they were reduced to the ranks, depending on the degree of insubordination and violence. Some commanding officers, such as Gen. Bradley, regarded the situation as so prejudicial to military discipline, that in 1878 he banned traders from approaching within five miles of his camps in the Black Hills.

Discipline

Few problems were more vexing to commanders than that of maintaining discipline. The problem of desertion has already been touched upon. It was never satisfactorily solved, although the improvements in living conditions, pay and food that came with the reforms of the late 1880s made considerable headway in reducing the number of desertions. The main problem, however, was caused by alcohol rather than the desire to abscond from the rigours of service life. Fights, abusive behaviour and insubordination were the inevitable results of over-indulgence, and the reaction of the Regular Army to such behaviour was often unnecessarily brutal. Justice was usually left to the company officers or senior NCOs, unless the case was particularly serious, in which case the commanding officer would pass judgement, or decide on a court martial. The rank and file had little faith in the impartiality of court martials, and when feasible, the accused man would usually vanish beforehand. Where discipline was left to the whim of the commanding officer, penalties could be unreasonably harsh. George Custer was a strict disciplinarian,

bordering on a martinet, and tolerated no slackness in the 7th Cavalry. Punishments meted out included bucking and gagging (being in a crouched position, with the ankles tied, and wrists fastened to a wooden rod that passed behind the knees), and confinement in an earthen guardhouse with no windows, and a roof too low to permit vertical movement. He illegally instructed one search party to shoot any deserters found. Two were indeed brought back slung over their saddles, the good colonel being subsequently severely censured for the order.

Other officers had a more humane approach, and did not condone unwarranted brutality by any soldier, regardless of rank, although in practice such acts were hard to detect. Fines or hard labour were the most common punishments levied. The loss of a month's wages was a serious blow to a trooper, curtailing his social life to virtually nothing, and such fines would be handed out for the most common of crimes – drunkenness, insubordination, neglection of duty or disobedience. Up to 1874 serious crimes such as murder, robbery and desertion would result in soldiers being confined to state penitentiaries under civilian jurisdiction. After 1874 the US Military prison at Fort Leavenworth was opened, where all military personnel were sent to serve their sentences.

Justice in the frontier army was often an arbitrary affair, and many soldiers of otherwise good character deserted after receiving unwarranted punishments for minor offences. It was only in 1891 that an order was prescribed limiting the punishments that a court martial could hand out. However, soldiers were no angels, and some idea of the level of offences can be gauged from a note appended in the Report of the Secretary of War, stating that 45 per cent of the command of the Department of the Missouri had been tried by the courts in that year!

Food

The rations supplied for the Army campaigning against the Indians were a typical example of Government under-funding. Ration food had never been spectacular in quality or quantity, but during the Civil War, most soldiers had been able to supplement their diet with meat, fruit and vegetables stolen along the way or purchased from post traders and local townspeople, who were only too happy to supply such a lucrative market. Parcels from home were a welcome addition, and most volunteer regiments had company funds upon which to draw to provide extra food when needed. For the most part, such luxuries were denied the troopers stationed in far-flung outposts. Standard rations comprised salt pork, range beef, coffee and hard tack (a solid biscuit, about 4 ins. × 4 ins., which could crack teeth if not softened first with water).

It is certainly true that transportation difficulties made supplying the posts a logistical nightmare. Food, ammunition and clothes had to be hauled by wagon from the nearest rail-heads, usually across miles of hostile country. The teamsters who rode the wagons were tough, brave and determined to profit from their labours. Apart from rations, they brought in barrels of potatoes, apples, onions, butter and eggs. In 1867, at Fort C.F. Smith, it would cost a trooper $2 a pound for butter and $15 (a little over a month's wages) for a bushel of potatoes. Fresh vegetables and dairy produce were not supplied by the Government, and it was not until the late 1880s that canned vegetables were supplied. Occasionally a dried potato or vegetable cake was issued, which when added to water produced a weak soup, but it was not popular. Initially no field cooks were appointed, so men usually took turns at preparing food which was often a recipe for gastronomic disaster! Food was usually boiled, or fried if fat was available, and the skillet was employed for each and every occasion. A system of appointing company cooks was gradually adopted, which was an improvement greatly appreciated by the enlisted men.

Soldiers would forage for anything available, and settlers' pigs, goats and chickens were fair game. Vegetable gardens were popular and encouraged at posts, and these made a valuable nutritional supplement to the diet of the men. Diet-related diseases such as scurvy would occur in poorly supplied outposts, despite the best efforts of officers and men to vary their diet. (During the Sioux Campaign of 1876, Col. Gibbons' column suffered badly from scurvy.) Much of the issue food was left over from the Civil War. In 1866, Pvt. W. Murphy wrote, 'I believe the bacon would have killed the men if it had not been thoroughly boiled ... [it was] yellow with age and

Fort Davis, Texas, circa 1885. Barely comparable with the early forts, Davis was the home to several Cavalry regiments, whose troopers gave sterling service against the South-western tribes. (Fort Davis National Historical Site)

bitter as quinine.' Flour was no better, often delivered short measured in sacks with weights in them to make up the loss. One trooper commented, 'The flour had been hauled 65 miles and handled several times. The result was that the refuse left by the mice was well mixed with the flour and we found a number of dead mice in it also. One reason why our rations were so scanty was that the flour was worth $100 a sack.'

Coffee, the staple drink of all US soldiers, was issued green. Beans were roasted over a fire and pounded into granules, usually with the butt of a pistol. Hardtack was useful when it was correctly cooked. Crushed and mixed with fat and bacon, it could be fried, or turned into a form of pudding if boiled in water with stewed prunes or apples.

Not surprisingly, even in the 1880s war-manufactured food was still being issued. Eighth Cavalryman Williamson wrote that 'some of the hardtack . . . was packed in 1863 . . . the hardtack had a green mould on it, but we just wiped it off and they were all right. Most anything tasted good.' Sometimes a remote dwelling would furnish luxuries, such as the small store in Dakota whose proprietress sold cakes and pies. So popular were they that sweet-toothed cavalrymen borrowed from their comrades at $2 for $1 just to sample a pie.

An important addition to the diet was wild game shot by hunting parties – deer, buffalo, wild turkey, jackrabbits, racoon and even prairie dogs were all welcome additions to the pot for a hungry soldier. David Spotts said that when rations had run out, some men tried mule meat, but it tasted foul. After

A typical interior of a barracks in the late 1880s. This was Fort Robinson, but could well have been any fort of the period. Foot lockers, wardrobes, a stove, pool table and weapons rack promise organisation and comforts only dreamed of two decades earlier. (National Archives)

two weeks 'on air and water', he came upon the bivouac of fellow 19th Volunteer Cavalry troopers: 'Gus [gave me] a cigar . . . I put it in my mouth and chewed it. I told them . . . I would like something to eat. They soon had plenty before me, but I could only eat a cracker and drink a cup of coffee, and that was enough to make me sick for a while'.

COMBAT AND TACTICS

Active service was usually a relief from the monotony of post life. As one Indian campaigner wrote, 'The only real romance in the West is chasing Indians, but fighting them is another story'. Indeed, of the thousands of miles marched by US troops in the West, few actually resulted in contact with the wily enemy. This was partly due to the methods of warfare adopted by the two sides. Army tactics, dating from the 18th century, called for set-piece battles by massed opposing forces. Having established their positions, the two sides would blaze away at each other until one vacated the field. The tactics of the Civil War were hardly different from Crècy, the Hundred Years War or the epic Napoleonic battles. True, the use of firearms had increased distances, and the Cavalry were used less as a battering ram, and more to skirmish, scout and harass supply lines, but the essential method of fighting was the same. To the Indian, this was a total anathema. Indian culture, particularly that of the Plains Indians, placed a very high regard upon personal bravery, and Indians almost never acted as a coherent, commanded fighting unit. When they did, as the Nez Percé and Modocs illustrated, they could prove to be formidable adversaries.

The end result of most campaigns in which cavalrymen found themselves involved was hunger, exhaustion, worn-out horses and equipment, and not more than a fleeting glimpse of Indian scouts keeping a wary eye on the troopers. Private D. Spotts of the 19th Kansas Volunteer Cavalry trekked from Topeka, near Kansas City, south to Fort Sill in Oklahoma, then north to Camp Supply on the Oklahoma/Texas border and up to Fort Hays in West Kansas, between October 1868 and April 1869,

without actually engaging any hostile Indians. Most military contact resulted from lightning attacks on parties of reinforcements, supply wagons and, in particular, fatigue parties, as one wood-cutting party found out in September 1866 at Piney Island, near Fort Phil Kearney. A dozen troopers were working on the timberline when 100 Indians appeared without warning and tried to cut off the party, who sprinted towards a log blockhouse built for such an eventuality. All made it save a Pvt. Smith, who was riddled with arrows and scalped, but astonishingly managed to crawl half a mile to the blockhouse, after snapping off the arrows in his body, to stop them snagging on the undergrowth. His fate is not recorded.

Indian motives for attack were complex. Sometimes they would ignore farmers they regarded as friendly, and massacre the inhabitants of the next dwelling. In other instances, they would murder randomly and seemingly without provocation. In the West, the reason was usually revenge for the unwarranted attacks by settlers and miners who occupied the land, quite often in open contravention of Government Treaties, and treated the native Indians as vermin. In other cases, young braves would launch attacks simply through boredom or a need to prove their manhood.

In the South-west, Kiowa, Navaho, Apache and Comanche raids were less as a result of infiltration by whites, than an intense and consuming hatred of Mexicans. In fact, the Apache chiefs, Mangas Colorados and Cochise, had not been hostile to Americans until 1861 when a misunderstanding over Apache raids led to a series of revenge killings that threw the South-west into turmoil.

Attempting to catch raiding bands was, as one soldier put it, 'Like trying to catch the wind'. In the west, Sioux and Cheyenne would melt into the vastness of the plains, using their intimate knowledge of the ravines, mountains and rivers. Apache and other Mexican border tribes headed for the gaunt and forbidding protection of the Chisos or Chiricahua mountains, or the arid deserts. Even using Indian scouts, the Cavalry often found that instead of being the hunters, they were the hunted. 'The entire detachment was in this dry bed urging the teams through the sand, when to our complete astonishment, a volley of arrows and rifle shots were poured into us. The shots were accompanied with a chorus of savage yells and the timberland and brush above and about us was fairly alive with Indians,' wrote an exasperated Mrs Carrington, an officer's wife.

Many officers who served in the West had the dual disadvantages of a Civil War military education, which was sadly lacking in practical application where Indians were concerned, and a deep-rooted attitude of racial superiority. One of the finest examples in this tradition was Capt. Fetterman, an over-confident Civil War veteran, who had often boasted that given 80 men, he could defeat the whole Sioux nation. He fell for the simplest and most often tried of all Indian tricks, the decoy. On a freezing day on 21 December 1866, ironically along with exactly 80 men of the 2nd Cavalry, he chased a small band of warriors into an ambush of over 2,000 armed warriors. There were no survivors.

How soldiers reacted in combat varied widely. Companies with seasoned veterans in them drew strength from their coolness under fire. During Crooks' pursuit of the Sioux in 1876, a 5th Cavalry rearguard was surprised when the ridge around them suddenly became alive with warriors. Some of the men began to panic and fire into the air, but as Capt. Charles King observed, they were calmed by 'a stalwart bearded fellow commanding the right skirmishers of the company . . . never bending himself, he moves from point to point cautioning such new hands as are excitedly throwing away their shots. He is their first sergeant, a crack soldier'.

Indian attitudes to warfare

It is important to understand the psychology of the men faced with meeting the Indian in combat, for the normal rules of European warfare did not apply. Indians regarded the life of a captured enemy as forfeit, and humane treatment of military prisoners was rare unless they were held for hostage purposes. Indian warriors gained much status from their ability to withstand pain, and trained themselves from youth to bear wounds and injury without complaint. A captive who was tortured to death was held in high esteem if he failed to show pain. Soldiers, however, found this as abhorrent as the Indian practice of

mutilating the dead, which was done to prevent the spirit entering heaven, rather than as a means of desecration. All soldiers dreaded capture, and experienced Indian fighters always had one piece of advice for new recruits, 'Never let them catch you alive – keep the last bullet for yourself'. There is evidence that this was heeded in several instances. During the Fetterman fight, the two surviving officers, their ammunition almost exhausted, placed their revolvers against each other's temples and pulled the triggers. Similar sights were witnessed during the Little Big Horn battle, several warriors later reporting that some troopers had gone crazy and shot themselves. Amos Bad Heart Bull, an Oglala Sioux, who fought at the battle, recounted how a mounted Cavalry sergeant, drawing away from braves who were chasing him, suddenly placed his revolver to his head and killed himself. Pvt. Peter Thompson of the 7th Cavalry, one of Reno's men who survived the subsequent siege, stated categorically, 'I made up my mind that all but one shot would be fired at the Indians and that one would go into my own head for I had determined never to be taken alive.'

Such desperate and decisive actions as fought by Fetterman and Custer were the exception. Generally, engagements were swift and inconsequential, resulting in a few casualties on each side. When surprised by a group of Modocs in May 1873, 5th Cavalrymen

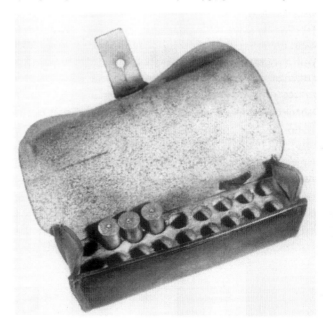

Infantry cartridge pouch modified to hold .50-70 cartridges for use in converted Sharps carbines. (Author's collection)

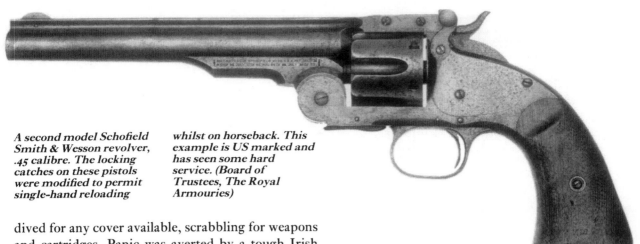

A second model Schofield Smith & Wesson revolver, .45 calibre. The locking catches on these pistols were modified to permit single-hand reloading whilst on horseback. This example is US marked and has seen some hard service. (Board of Trustees, The Royal Armouries)

dived for any cover available, scrabbling for weapons and cartridges. Panic was averted by a tough Irish sergeant, Kelly, who leaped up and yelled, 'God damn it, let's charge ...' The troopers killed five Modocs without suffering any casualties. Set-piece battles between massed opposing forces were very rare, one exception being the battle of the Rosebud on 17 June 1876, when the 1,000-strong column of Gen. Crook met with a similar number of Sioux and Cheyenne. The battle raged for six hours until the Indians withdrew. Crook claimed a victory, but his soldiers had been badly mauled and were forced to return to their supply base.

Most fighting was not done on equal terms, invariably one side outnumbered the others and many 'battles' claimed as victories for the Army were not battles at all, but bloody, one-sided attacks on Indian camps. One example was the Sand Creek massacre of 1868, when 700 volunteer cavalrymen, under a maniacal colonel called Chivington, attacked the peaceful Cheyenne camp of Chief Black Kettle killing 123 men, women and children. George Custer achieved a similar result in the battle of the Washita, when his men attacked another Cheyenne camp. As Capt. A. Barnitz wrote, the cavalrymen came 'crashing through the frozen snow as the troops deployed into line at a gallop and the Indian village rang with unearthly war whoops, the quick discharge of firearms ... the cries of infants and the wailing of women'. In this instance, they met stiff resistance and suffered 19 killed and 14 wounded. Black Kettle and his wife, who had escaped from Sand Creek, were shot down by the cavalrymen.

For the soldiers, such flashes of excitement rarely enlivened their endless trekking across prairie and desert. The men were not politicians or tacticians, and few held any personal animosity against the Indians, often believing them to be victims of circumstance rather than inherently evil. There is no doubt that they feared them, and exposure to Indian methods of killing and mutilation hardened attitudes, but the reaction of troopers to the Indian also depended to a great extent on where they served and their experiences. After Little Big Horn, the 7th Cavalry became renowned as a regiment that hated Indians, finally wreaking their revenge at Wounded Knee in 1890. Units who fought the Nez Percé and Utes invariably held their fighting qualities in high regard, and were more inclined to treat captives kindly. The 6th Cavalry, who had fought a long campaign against the Apache in 1885 in some of the most rugged and inhospitable terrain anywhere on earth, were impressed at the Indians' ability to live and fight in such a land, and upon the surrender of the Apache leader, Nana, expressed open astonishment that the wizened old man could have outwitted the Army for so long.

Much of what the soldiers believed about Indians had come from the mawkish, sentimental and racially biased literature of the period. Mostly they were portrayed as blood-thirsty savages with no morals and little intelligence, except an animal cunning. Many soldiers were intelligent enough to query this view, though some believed that Sherman's dictum, 'the only good Indian is a dead one', was a reasonable viewpoint, particularly if they had witnessed the aftermath of Indian attacks. Long service during the

Indian wars tended to modify ingrained prejudices, and it was clear to many soldiers that white greed and ignorance was the cause of much trouble. Few trusted the Indian Bureau, who kept the reservation Indians supplied, and whose crooked agents often short-changed them, issuing sub-standard food and clothing in place of the issue rations, which they subsequently sold. Sgt. George Neihaus, having fought the Apache, summed up the attitude of many troopers, 'The Indians were promised lots of things, and they were betrayed: then the Indians went out to raid the settlers. I feel the Indian agents, many times – not all – were the cause of a great deal of unrest.'

WOUNDS AND SICKNESS

The rigours of campaign life and the isolation of frontier posts when combined with the limitations of medical science conspired against a soldier unlucky enough to become ill or wounded. Common ailments and diseases were survivable with luck and a convenient hospital. TB and venereal diseases were the most usual afflictions, but cholera and dysentery could decimate a garrison, as Albert Barnitz mentioned in a letter to his wife on 20 July 1867, 'Only think, seven dead men in an evening (all of the 7th Cavalry) isn't a small beginning at all . . . and more the following day. I would much rather see two Indians than one man with the cholera and I am not remarkably fond of Indians either!'

Hygiene was basic and, although the men were expected to bathe weekly, this was often impossible in garrisons where every barrel of water had to be brought in by wagon. Poor sanitation and a tendency to drink any water available when on patrol led to frequent stomach ailments. Most serious cases would be admitted to the post hospital, where if they had a strong constitution and a lot of luck, they might survive to be placed on light duty until eventually recovered.

For those wounded in fights with the Indians, the chances of survival were equally capricious. Bullets of the period were an unpleasant combination of large calibre and soft lead, so a wound anywhere other than a soft, fleshy part of the body was likely to prove serious, with shattered bones and infection being the result. Amputation was the usual treatment for arms and legs, although occasionally skilful nursing would save the limb, albeit leaving the owner with limited use. Indian arrowheads were long and made of thin, soft sheet steel, which deformed badly upon striking a bone. The usual method of removal was to slide a loop of wire along the shaft into the wound, hook the

Soldiers at Fort Keogh in winter 1886. They wear buffalo coats and seal or muskrat hats and gloves. The man on the extreme left has a webbing cartridge belt over his coat. (Little Bighorn Battlefield National Monument)

arrow tip onto the loop, and withdraw both. Peritonitis and gangrene would frequently set in, although a clean wound could heal remarkably quickly. Lance thrusts were invariably deep and fatal, but men could survive apparently fatal gunshot wounds as Albert Barnitz proved. Shot at point blank range by an Indian with a .56 or .70 calibre musket, the ball '... struck the lower edge of a rib, and then glancing downward, as I was leaning forward at the time, cut the next rib in two and a piece out of the next rib below where it reflected, and passed through my body and out through the muscle near the spine, passing again through my overcoat and cape'. Despite travelling 100 miles in an ambulance wagon, he recovered and eventually returned to duty. Indians habitually scalped their enemies, involving a circular incision from 2 to 10 ins. across, with the hair and flesh being unceremoniously yanked off. It was also possible to survive scalping, depending on the size of the scalp lifted, although constant headaches and an aversion to extremes of temperature were the usual result.

Statistically, there was more chance of becoming a casualty through illness than as a result of action, with eight men per 1,000 dying from disease, and five per 1,000 as a consequence of wounds, injuries or accidents. One of the most common accidents for cavalrymen was being thrown from their mounts. Trooper Ami Mulford, who wrote a classic account of life as a frontier cavalryman, was crushed by his horse, and discharged crippled at the age of 23. Another was accidental shooting, with most memoirs

covering service during the Indian Wars mentioning at least one death as a result of carelessness or fear.

The quality of Army doctors was questionable too, as the low pay was not likely to attract the more successful and competent. Medical orderlies were untrained, and often men of low ability whose inadequacies did not leave them fit for fighting service. After 1870, Congress exacerbated matters by reducing the number of medical officers from a barely adequate 222 to 192. Presumably none of the Congressmen had ever been forced to wait for a doctor to remove a deeply embedded arrow.

CAMPAIGNS

To understand the difficulties faced by the Army in Indian campaigning, four individual actions are used to illustrate how adaptable commanders had to be to fight and expect any chance of success. In no single instance can any of these actions be taken to be a military success as the modern military historian would understand it. All were gains or losses of a very limited nature, but they show how the Army responded over the period 1865–1890 to the challenge of guerilla warfare. Some commanders, such as Custer, continued with Civil War tactics, and never truly succeeded in fighting Indians on their own terms. Others, like Gen. Miles and Gen. Crook, learned to adapt their tactics to find and fight an elusive and cunning foe.

The Washita, 1868

The battle of Washita on 27 November 1868 is a fine example of traditional mounted tactics, which if used against any European foe, would doubtless have proved a resounding victory for the Cavalry. Throughout the summer, Gen. Phil Sheridan had developed a plan to strike at Indian camps when winter curtailed the warrior's ability to travel and fight. He sent two 'outrider' columns, comprising 3rd Cavalry and 37th Infantry under Maj. Gen. G.W. Getty, 5th Cavalry and 10th Cavalry under Maj. Carr

Another view of soldiers from Fort Keogh. Surviving mid-western winters without such protection led to frequent amputations; temperatures of −60° were not unknown. (Montana Historical Society)

1: Corporal, 1st US Cavalry, 1865
2: Enlisted man's boot, 1872 pattern
3: Enlisted man's Jefferson shoe
4: Civil War pattern holster

A

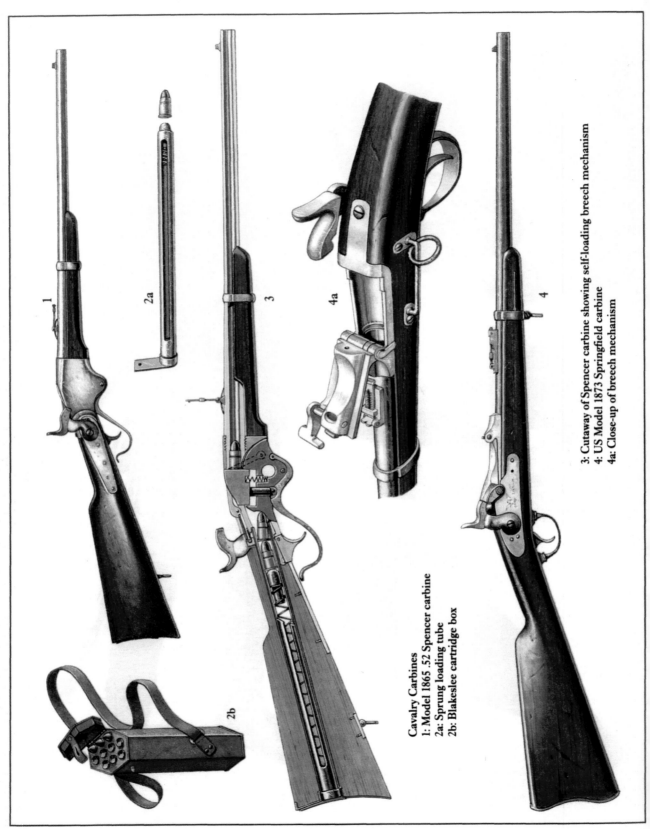

Cavalry Carbines
1: Model 1865 .52 Spencer carbine
2a: Sprung loading tube
2b: Blakeslee cartridge box
3: Cutaway of Spencer carbine showing self-loading breech mechanism
4: US Model 1873 Springfield carbine
4a: Close-up of breech mechanism

B

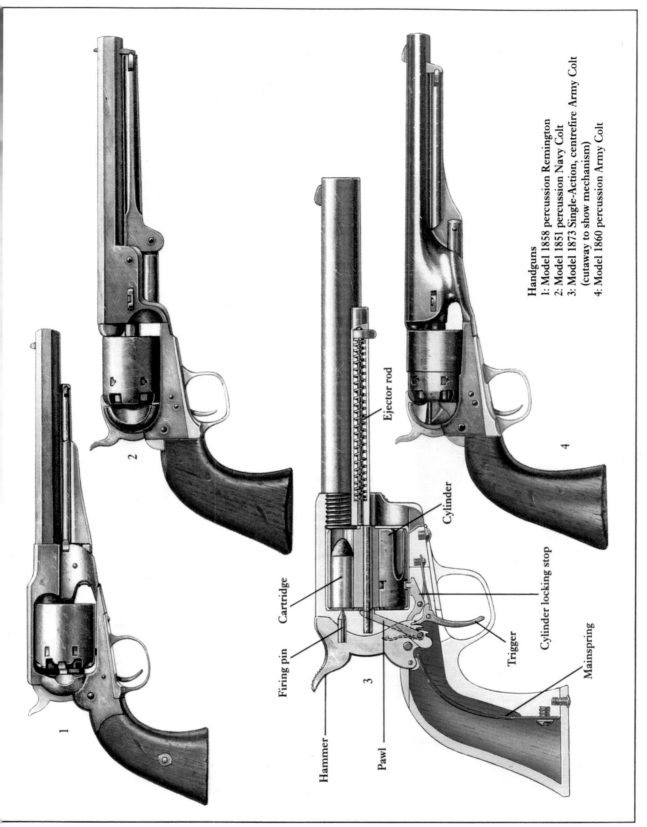

Handguns
1: Model 1858 percussion Remington
2: Model 1851 percussion Navy Colt
3: Model 1873 Single-Action, centrefire Army Colt (cutaway to show mechanism)
4: Model 1860 percussion Army Colt

Ejector rod

Cartridge

Cylinder

Firing pin

Cylinder locking stop

Hammer

Trigger

Pawl

Mainspring

1

2

3

4

C

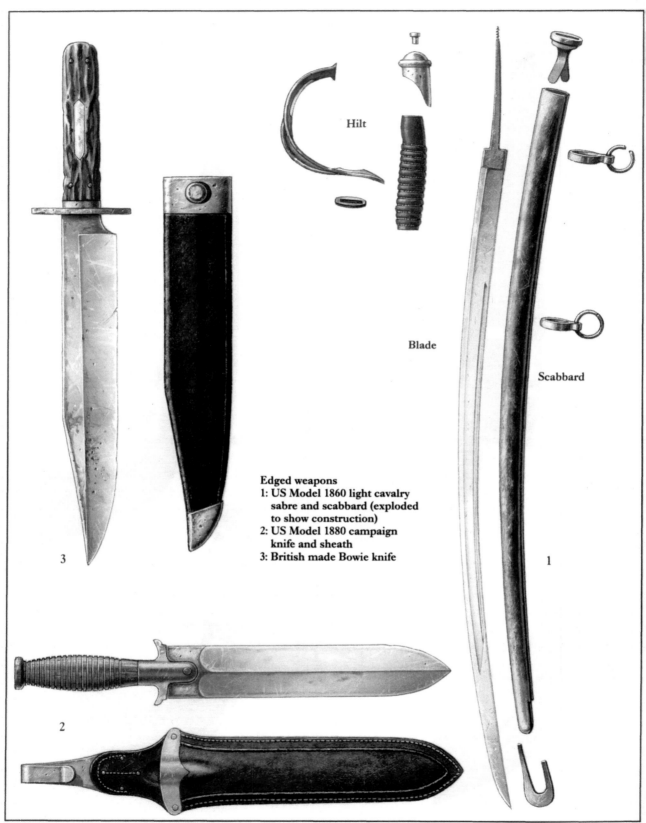

Hilt

Blade

Scabbard

Edged weapons
1: US Model 1860 light cavalry sabre and scabbard (exploded to show construction)
2: US Model 1880 campaign knife and sheath
3: British made Bowie knife

3

2

1

D

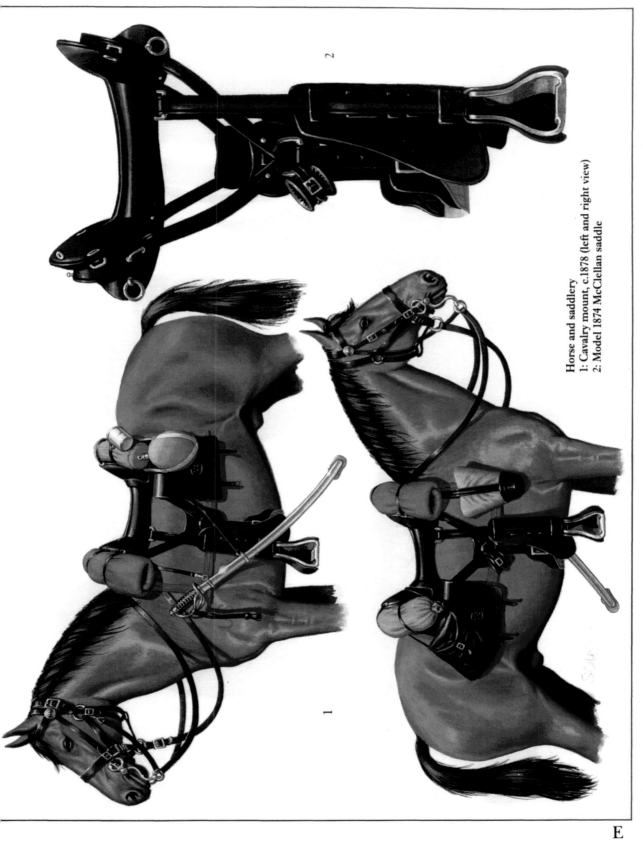

Horse and saddlery
1: Cavalry mount, c.1878 (left and right view)
2: Model 1874 McClellan saddle

E

1: Sergeant, US Cavalry, 1876
2: 1872 forage cap (exploded views)
3: 1855 Hardee hat
4: 1875 campaign hat

F

Cleaning and repair

G

Crook on campaign against the Apaches, Arizona, c.1873

H

Sabre practice, 1874

I

Mounted action, c.1874

J

Dismounted action, c.1885

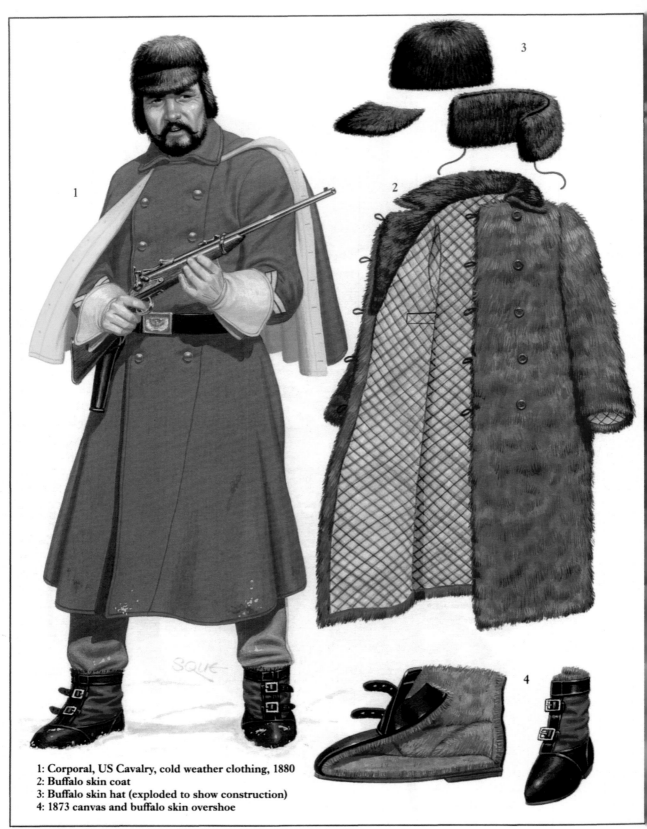

1: Corporal, US Cavalry, cold weather clothing, 1880
2: Buffalo skin coat
3: Buffalo skin hat (exploded to show construction)
4: 1873 canvas and buffalo skin overshoe

L

to drive the hostiles towards his own and Lt.Gen. Sully's column of 11 troops of 7th Cavalry, the 19th Kansas Volunteer Cavalry plus five companies of Infantry, the whole column comprising 800 men.

The pursuit had started badly, as the cold weather deteriorated into heavy, wet snow which lay a foot deep. Hampered by the weather and labouring supply wagons, plus much internal wrangling over command, Sheridan ordered Custer and the 7th Cavalry ahead of the column to try to pick up the hostile trail. After four hard days, during which the horses' grain issue was reduced from 12 to 3 lbs per day, the 7th came upon the Cheyenne camp nestled in a curve of the Washita River. Without ascertaining enemy strengths, or the possible location of other camps, Custer formed his men into four companies and charged. Initially, the attack appeared to have succeeded. Those Indians not killed abandoned the camp and disappeared into the surrounding woods. As the day progressed, the troopers found themselves under increasingly heavy fire from well concealed warriors, who had joined in the defence from a number of campsites spread along the valley, of which Custer had no knowledge. One Cavalry commander, Maj. J.H. Elliott, and 18 cavalrymen were cut off and killed, and Custer was forced to abandon the battlefield, with 21 dead and 14 wounded. The estimate of Indian dead is between ten and 20 warriors and 20 to 40 women and children. The loss of Elliott was to remain a blot on Custer's record for the rest of his service.

The real benefit of the Washita action was not to prove the value of Civil War battle tactics (used against Indians, they were something between wasteful and suicidal), but to prove the soundness of winter warfare. With their accompanying supply train, the cavalry and infantry could wage war at a time of year when Indians traditionally turned to more peaceful occupations. Loss of their campsites meant loss of shelter, foodstocks and horses, forcing them to make a choice – trek to a neighbouring campsite, if one existed, surrender and subsequent transportation to a reservation, or death from exposure or hunger.

Lava Beds, 1872–3

Of all the major actions fought by the Army in the West, this campaign against the Modocs led by Kintpuash proved what determined Indian resistance could accomplish, and gave the Army a chance to commit every military blunder in the book by underestimating the tenacity of their enemy, and overestimating the fighting ability of their own troops. For good measure, the terrain, which is probably unequalled in the United States for barren inhospitality, did not appear to figure largely in the minds of the commanders responsible for waging war on the Modocs.

Trouble had been brewing along the California–Oregon boundary since Kintpuash (also known as Captain Jack) had reluctantly signed a treaty with the US in 1864. The Modocs, Klamaths and Snakes had been moved to reservations, from which a year later the Modocs had moved back to their homelands. In 1872, Gen. Canby was instructed to forcibly return the Modocs – numbering no more than 70 men and their families – to the reservation. An attempt to do so by 40 regulars of the 1st Cavalry was met with a fusillade of gunfire. The result was one dead and one wounded Modoc, two dead and six wounded soldiers and the Indians vanished into lava beds known as the 'Stronghold'. This area comprised acres of jagged waves of frozen rock, full of caves, fissures and interconnecting labyrinths, and the Army was powerless to evict them. Reinforcements of 1st Cavalry and a detachment of 21st Infantry were brought in, as well as two 12 pdr. artillery guns. On the night of 16 January 1873, two attack columns under Maj. Green in the west and Capt. R.F. Bernard in the east edged towards the Stronghold, shrouded in fog. The artillerymen could see no targets and fired blindly, but splinters and rock fragments caused casualties to the troopers, so shelling was stopped. As the soldiers advanced, the silence was shattered by close, accurate fire from hidden Modocs, who probably understood the practical use of a rifle more than any other tribe, and could outshoot the average soldier. For the attacking soldiers, the world suddenly became a nightmare, as recalled in a letter by Lt. H.D. Moore: 'At first fire, the troops were so demoralised that officers could do nothing with them. Capt. Wright ordered his men to take possession of a bluff which would effectively secure their retreat but Capt. Wright was severely wounded ... and his company with one or two exceptions deserted him ... then the slaughter began.' Soldiers who remained at their posts fired

George Armstrong Custer in campaign dress for the Washita, 1869. With the exception of the rather fine buckskin jacket, he would have looked little different from his dusty and bearded troopers. (Little Bighorn Battlefield National Monument)

the Indians that caused their subsequent surrender when a breakaway group under a Shaman called Curley Headed Doctor led cavalrymen to the rebel camp. Kintpuash and three others were subsequently hanged for the murder of Canby at Fort Klamath.

Several lessons were learnt as a result of the campaign, the most important being that it required an Indian to catch an Indian. Scouts had always been employed by the Army, but valuable lives could be saved if renegade tribesmen were co-opted to fight. Once again the Army commanders totally underestimated the ability of their foe, and their attempts to take the Stronghold by direct assault were as foolhardy and wasteful as Polish Lancers attacking German tanks in 1940. Detailed reconnaissance, intimate knowledge of the terrain and adequate numbers of troops were all prerequisites for this form of campaigning which taught Gen. Sherman a costly lesson.

Big Dry Wash, 1882

The campaign in Arizona that culminated in the battle at Big Dry Wash was one of the longest running in the West. It is unusual on two accounts; it was one of the only times that the Army defeated the Apaches, and a rare instance of the Indians engaging in a nearly conventional battle.

Trouble with Apache bands, mainly White Mountain and Chiricahuas, had plagued the Mexican borders for years, but flared into violence over the killing of a Shaman named Nakaidoklini on 30 August 1881. Apache scouts mutinied, killing one officer and six men. Reinforcements of Cavalry served only to create an atmosphere of distrust among the reservation Chiricahua Indians, many of whom fled to join the White Mountain warriors. By the end of the year, Indian depredations had turned the Arizona–New Mexico area into a war zone, killing settlers and policemen, raiding farms and leaving upwards of 200 whites dead. These war parties were led by the most cunning guerilla leaders in history – Geronimo, Chato, Nachez, Juh and Chihuahua – and despite constant exhausting patrols, the cavalrymen had never glimpsed a sight of the hostiles. Some idea of conditions can be gained from the comments made by Surgeon L. Wood, attached to the 4th Cavalry, pursuing Apaches. Their horses had expired in the first week, they were reduced to 'marching every day

blindly, and none even saw an Indian during the entire engagement. The Army lost 11 dead and 26 wounded. The Stronghold was then ringed with bivouacs and observation posts, limiting Indian mobility and access to food and water. Subsequent peace talks failed when Kintpuash shot and killed Gen. Canby and two other peace commissioners. A second assault was launched, the unhappy cavalrymen again being forced to fight on foot. For three days between 15–17 April, two columns slowly advanced through the Stronghold and the Modocs would open fire and then melt away in organised retreat. An advance force under Capt. E. Thomas, of five officers and 59 men, were ambushed in a well-organised attack that claimed the lives of all the officers, 20 men and left 16 wounded. By the time the Army took the Stronghold, there were no Modocs in residence. Ironically, it was internal dissent amongst

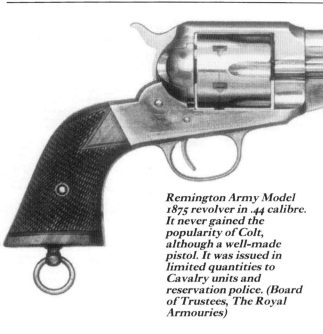

Remington Army Model 1875 revolver in .44 calibre. It never gained the popularity of Colt, although a well-made pistol. It was issued in limited quantities to Cavalry units and reservation police. (Board of Trustees, The Royal Armouries)

in that intense heat, the rocks and earth being so torrid that the feet are blistered and rifle barrels and everything metallic being so hot that the hand cannot touch them without getting burnt. . . . The rain when it does come, comes as a tropical tempest, transforming the dry canyons into raging torrents in an instant. We had no tents and little or no baggage of any kind except rations and ammunition. Suits of underclothing formed our uniform and moccasins covered our feet.'

After an inconclusive engagement at Horseshoe Canyon between the 4th Cavalry and the Apaches on 23 April, another command, comprising 14 troops of 3rd and 6th Cavalry and a number of Apache scouts commanded by Gen. Chaffee spotted a large body of Apaches under Chief Natiotish in an ambush position on the rim of a canyon. The Indians were engaged with fire, whilst four cavalry troops and some scouts encircled the hostiles, striking at both flanks. The battle raged all day, from dawn to 6 pm, the Indians well concealed but unable to retreat, the troopers working their way forward in the heat and dust from rock to rock, drawing Indian fire until sharpshooters could pick them off. Upwards of 25 Indians died, and it was believed by the attacking troops that none escaped unwounded. Good field command and sound tactics and training had paid off in this instance, but the fact that the Apaches were

forced to fight a pitched battle was a material factor in the success of the Army. It was to take another four years to finally subdue the Apache tribes.

Wounded Knee, 1890

The battle at Wounded Knee has been viewed from many angles, and dubbed a 'senseless massacre' by some historians. It should be borne in mind, however, that the Miniconjou Sioux camped on the Cheyenne River were by no means a settled reservation tribe. Many had been inflamed by the promises of the Ghost Dance, of a new world free of pain and hunger and empty of white men. Some of the radicals such as Kicking Bear and Short Bull took this to mean the destruction of the whites, and the Brulés and Oglala tribes became so aggressive and anarchical that the Indian Bureau panicked, demanding immediate reinforcements. Times had changed in the West over the previous decade. Forts now ringed reservation land, and well-supplied troops could be moved around by railroad. It was ironic that it should have been the 7th Cavalry (who had suffered so grievously at the hands of the Sioux in 1876) who were rushed to intercept the fleeing Chief Big Foot, who they mistakenly believed was leading his Miniconjous to meet with the Oglalas and Brulés. On the morning of 29 December 1890, the 350 Indians awoke to find themselves surrounded by 500 cavalrymen, armed with two quick-firing Hotchkiss guns. Neither side expected a fight, but all were tense, as the order was given for the Sioux to be disarmed. Many hid their guns under their clothing, and when a rifle went off accidentally, chaos ensued. Many troopers closest to the Indians took to their heels, leaving their horses to their own devices. Capt. George Wallace's skull was shattered by a point-blank rifle bullet, as both sides fought in hand-to-hand combat, using pistols, knives and rifle butts. Big Foot, ill with pneumonia, rose to watch and was instantly shot down. Some warriors armed with

Troop C, 3rd Cavalry, at Fort Davis, Texas, 1886. A fine photograph showing troopers in regulation uniforms, and still equipped with sabres, a rare sight by this date.

They wear 1883 campaign hats, and 1884 fatigue blouses, and carry Schofield Smith & Wesson revolvers. (Fort Davis National Historical Site)

Winchesters pumped shot after shot into the confused ranks of troopers. Meanwhile, the soldiers and Hotchkiss gunners on the ridge opened fire, adding to the uproar with the sharp crack of exploding shells. Many troopers across the rim of the hollow were struck by their comrades' bullets, and some closest to the Indians were injured by the shells. After an hour, the shooting subsided as the surviving Sioux fled. One hundred and fifty Indians, including 62 women and children, were killed and 50 wounded. Army losses were 25 officers and men, and 37 wounded.

As a battle, like most that occurred during the Indian Wars, Wounded Knee achieved little in purely military terms. The repercussions could have had disastrous consequences for the Army, for there were over 1,000 armed warriors in camps nearby, and violence seemed inevitable. Fortunately for both sides, Gen. Miles was in overall command, and his understanding of Indian psychology prevented what could have been a disastrous situation. By playing on the divided factions within the Sioux camp, he persuaded them to surrender their weapons. He promised food and shelter for the coming winter, whilst increasing the number of troops around the villages, a careful blend of carrot and stick. Incensed but frightened by the events at Wounded Knee, the Sioux gradually realised there was nothing to be gained by resistance, and they began to drift towards the Agency. On 21 January 1891, Miles's army formed up in procession, and to the sound of 'Garry Owen', the 7th Cavalry's marching song, left the valley. On the hills in the bitter wind, wrapped in blankets and buffalo robes, hundreds of Sioux watched silently as their way of life went with them.

SITES OF INTEREST

Big Bend National Park, Southern Texas
On the edge of the Rio Grande, the park was the base for generations of Kiowa, Comanche and Apache raiders. The landscape is brutal, and unchanged since the years of the Indian Wars.

Big Hole Battlefield, Wisdom, Montana
The site of the clash between Col. John Gibbon and the Nez Percé under Chief Joseph in August 1877.

Buffalo Bill Historic Center, Cody, Wyoming
A wonderful collection of weapons, Indian artefacts and ephemera.

Custer Battlefield, Hardin, Montana
The desolate battle site where Custer and 225 men died on 25 June 1876. There is an excellent museum on the site, and a large graveyard where the victims of the Indian Wars from all over the West are buried.

Fort Abraham Lincoln, Mandan, North Dakota
The base for many expeditions into the Black Hills and the fort from where Custer led his men to the Little Big Horn, and the Cavalry pursued Chief Joseph.

Fort Bowie, Bowie, Arizona
In the remote Apache Pass, this fort was the base for the patrols and larger military operations against the Apaches, directed by Gen. Crook and Gen. Miles.

Fort Buford, Buford, North Dakota
From 1866 to 1870, the fort was the centre of the most

hostile Indian territory in the West. It was here that Sitting Bull and Gall surrendered after the Little Big Horn. Some original buildings survive and there is a museum.

Fort Davis, Fort Davis, Texas
The base for the Black 9th and 10th Cavalry operating against Apache raiders, the fort has been partially restored and has an extensive programme of living history during the summer months.

Fort Sill, Lawton, Oklahoma
An important post of the Indian Wars, particularly during the Red River Wars 1874–5. It is the burial place of such eminent chiefs as Geronimo, Satanta, Satank and Quanah Parker.

Fort Union, Watrons, New Mexico
Built on the Santa Fe trail in 1851, it was a major supply base for 40 years for campaigns against the

south-western tribes. A museum is in the ruins and living history is enacted during the summer months.

Lava Beds National Monument, Tulelake, California
The heartland of the Modoc Wars, this inhospitable terrain shows the formidable task faced by the Army trying to defeat Captain Jack during the six-month campaign waged there.

Lower Sioux Agency and Fort Ridgely, Redwood Falls, Minnesota
Site of the Sioux uprising in 1862 that sparked off years of bloody conflict. The Agency has a museum telling the story, and the fort, which was the base to many hard-pressed army units, is close by.

Nez Percé National Historical Park, Idaho
A large area comprising 23 different sites, showing the history of conflict between the settlers and Nez Percé culminating in the war of 1877.

Wounded Knee Battlefield, Pine Ridge, South Dakota
Markers and a mass grave plot the tragic end to the Indian Wars. An emotive and poignant place.

PLATES

A1: Corporal, 1st US Cavalry, 1865
A cavalryman at the end of the Civil War. He wears the useless 'bummer' cap, an item of headgear heartily disliked by the troopers, and replaced whenever possible by a more practical and comfortable slouch hat. His shell jacket is as issued, but for comfort many men wore the collar turned down, and cut the pointed front of the jacket away. He carries issue weapons – a percussion pistol (troopers often had up to six revolvers with them when in battle) and a Spencer carbine, into which he is loading a new magazine tube. The Spencer was a popular rifle, and the cavalryman valued its repeating capability. The sabre, although a much prized symbol, was of little practical use to a trooper, and after the early 1870s was seldom carried into action.

A2: Enlisted man's boot, 1872 pattern
An exploded illustration of the high-leg 1872 boot. They could be worn on either foot, being virtually indistinguishable left from right. Some manufacturers were better than others, but on campaign a pair of boots seldom lasted more than four weeks. Soles could be sewn or screwed to the uppers, but after repeated soakings and drying in front of fires, even the most solidly constructed boot would disintegrate.

A3: Enlisted man's Jefferson Shoe
These were rarely worn on campaign after the Civil War, as they did not give adequate protection to the legs and feet in the thick brush of the West. In the south-western deserts, the spines of some cacti could actually penetrate leather. The shoe was mainly worn off-duty or during fatigues, and stocks of wartime shoes were still being issued in the 1880s.

A4: Civil War pattern holster
A practical leather holster, well liked by troopers, and often found in use up to 1890. Originally made for percussion revolvers, it was modified by soldiers to accept the later centrefire pistols, usually by simply adding another securing stud, or increasing the length of the securing tab to accommodate the slightly bulkier Colt or Smith & Wesson .45.

B: Cavalry Carbines
B1: Model 1865 .52 Spencer carbine
Cavalrymen could not easily operate a full length rifle, which was heavy and unwieldly when fighting on horseback, so carbines were issued which used the same cartridge as an infantry rifle, but were shorter and lighter. Usually the hook of the carbine sling could be attached to the weapon, to avoid it being lost in combat. The Spencer was the first ever repeating carbine adopted into military service. Troopers liked its rate of fire, but found the rimfire cartridge underpowered, and liable to misfire.

B2a: Sprung loading tube
This shows the sprung loading tube, which enabled seven cartridges to be retained in the butt of the carbine. To release the trooper simply twisted the steel plate (visible on the left) through 45°, and pulled the tube out of the butt.

B2b: Blakeslee cartridge box
Some cavalry units were issued with Blakeslee cartridge boxes, which held ten ready-loaded tubes,

each of which could rapidly be emptied into the butt. They were a practical, if expensive, solution to the problem of carrying the soft copper cartridges without damaging them, and those units who received them appeared to have held them in high regard.

B3: Cutaway of Spencer carbine showing self-loading breech mechanism

This illustration of the Spencer shows the magazine tube in place with two cartridges waiting to be used. Operation was simple: the cocking lever beneath the trigger was lowered, allowing the breech block to drop. This enabled the coiled spring in the magazine tube to push a cartridge over the top of the block and into the breech. At the same time, a hinged bar automatically slid the hammer back. Once the lever was closed, the carbine was cocked and ready to fire, as is the example illustrated here. The major problem encountered by the troopers was dust and grit clogging the mechanism, preventing the breech from closing. In desert conditions, the guns would not be oiled, as this would attract dirt.

B4: US Model 1873 Springfield carbine

The Springfield was the successor to the Spencer and Sharps carbines; though many regarded the 'Trap-

Another view of 'Troop C'. Carbines are Springfields, and an assortment of belts are worn, including early leather sabre belts with eagle buckles, 1881 and 1885 Mills cartridge belts and one or two plain leather cartridge loops. At least two troopers carry knives. The officer in the foreground wears a straw hat. (Fort Davis National Historical Site)

door' Springfield as a backward step, since it was only capable of single-shot operation, having to be reloaded by hand before each subsequent shot. Its .45 calibre centrefire cartridge was more accurate than the old .52 rimfire, with a slightly greater range. It was a very simple and durable weapon, and served the cavalry from 1873 to the 1890s.

B4a: Close-up of the breech mechanism

Many thousands of Civil War Springfields were converted to the Allin breechloading system. This meant cutting the rear of the breech off, and replacing it with a hinged section which was released by means of a thumb latch. When open, a cartridge could be inserted, the breech was snapped shut, and the hammer manually cocked. Once fired, the catch was released, the block raised and a small ejector pushed the fired case to the rear. In practice, black powder fouling, verdigris and dirt often combined to glue the case firmly in the breech, leaving the unhappy trooper to dig the case out with a knife. If this happened in the midst of a battle, the results could be fatal, and it has been the basis of one explanation for the destruction of Custer's command at the Little Big Horn in 1876.

C: Handguns

C1: Model 1858 percussion Remington

A robust .44 calibre pistol that saw much service during the Civil War and Indian Wars. It was a particular favourite of Indian braves, who used captured examples with enthusiasm. Its solid frame made it less susceptible to damage than the Colts, and it was generally well-liked.

C2: Model 1851 percussion Navy Colt

Manufactured in large numbers for over two decades, the .36 Navy was probably the most common percussion revolver in the west. Although reliable enough, it suffered from the same problem as the .44 Army (No. 4) in that the barrel was only held in place by a steel wedge retained in the cylinder axis pin. The small bullet lacked the power of the bigger .44, and had an effective killing range of only about 25 yards.

C3: Model 1873 Single-Action, centrefire Army Colt

Like the other revolvers illustrated here, the Colt was a single-action pistol, requiring manual cocking for each shot. However, it was the first cartridge revolver adopted by the US Army, and proved to be a reliable and practicable weapon. Cartridges were loaded one at a time through a spring-loaded gate on the right of

First Sgt., John Comfort, 4th Cavalry, in 1877. He wears virtually no issue clothing. His 'sailor' shirt, hat and neckerchief are privately purchased, as apparently are his boots.

His belt is an issue leather one with home-made canvas loops attached. Just visible on his left hip is a large knife. (US Signal Corps)

the frame, behind the cylinder. Cocking the hammer lifted the pawl which engaged in small slots at the rear of the cylinder. This forced the cylinder to rotate one-sixth of a revolution, lining up a cartridge with the barrel. The locking stop then engaged in a slot in the cylinder to ensure that alignment remained perfect. The trigger could then be pulled to fire the gun. A drawback was the slowness of ejecting, which had to be done one case at a time, using a spring-loaded rod in the ejector tube. The .45 calibre bullet was a real man-stopper, however, and in steady hands the pistol was accurate up to 50 yards. So popular was the Colt that it remained in constant production until 1940.

C4: Model 1860 percussion Army Colt

A .44 calibre version of the Navy Colt, it was preferred by cavalrymen because of its larger bullet and greater power. Along with the Navy Colt, it suffered from frame weakness, and if used as a club (not uncommon in hand to hand fighting) it could bend so badly as to be unfireable. Most troopers carried at least a pair of percussion pistols and often several spare loaded cylinders, to save time reloading, which involved filling each chamber with powder, then ramming a lead bullet in using a lever underneath the barrel. A percussion cap then had to be fitted to the nipples at the rear of the cylinder – no easy task in the heat of battle or if one had cold hands.

D: Edged Weapons
D1: US Model 1860 light cavalry sabre and scabbard

The steel scabbard is made in one piece, rolled and then brazed closed, with suspension loops and end shoe also brazed into place. A sprung steel collar fits into the neck of the scabbard, and helps to hold the blade in place. The blade is forged in one piece, with the wooden grip, brass guard and pommel all held in place by a rivet. It was of questionable use in the field, being issued unsharpened, but was undoubtedly a status symbol for cavalrymen. Cumbersome and noisy, it was invariably left behind when on campaign.

D2: US Model 1880 campaign knife and sheath

A heavy-bladed, well-made knife with turned wooden grip and brass-mounted leather sheath, this was the first campaign knife issued to the Cavalry, who lacked any form of practical knife for day to day use. It was a tool with myriad uses from opening cans to cutting leather to replace broken harness or equipment. It was even pressed into service as a fighting knife, though few troopers were as adept at using it as the Indians.

A Cavalry officer at Fort Wingate, New Mexico, circa 1886. He wears a shortened 1876 sack coat and has Apache style leggings. His 1881 Mills belt has the 'H' shaped cast brass buckle. He also wears a hunting knife. His hat and neckerchief are not issue items. (Museum of New Mexico)

D3: British-made Bowie knife

A typical Bowie-bladed weapon, with its distinctive, tapering, false-edged blade, it is a design that can be traced back to the Anglo-Saxon 'scramasax' knife. Many thousands of similar knives were exported to the United States during the latter half of the 19th century, and the example illustrated represents one of the slightly better-quality versions available. It has horn grips and nickel fittings, with an inlaid silver escutcheon in the left grip. The blade is Sheffield steel. The sheath is leather with a silver chape and locket. It could be carried from a leather loop hung on a belt, or simply tucked into the waistband, while some troopers preferred to slide it into a boot top. Virtually every man carried a knife of some sort and it is surprising that the Army did not issue one officially until 1880.

E: Horse and saddlery
E1: Cavalry mount c.1870 (left and right views)

The curb bridle, McClellan saddle and saddlebags are all regulation issue for 1874. This mount is carrying the equipment as officially issued – the blanket roll is carried on the front of the saddle, with rolled forage sack strapped to the rear. The upper illustration shows the sabre slung from its straps and a canteen and cup attached to the rear. The lower illustration shows the trooper's haversack hung from the saddlebag, whilst forward of the saddle is the nosebag. In practice, troopers carried additional gear if the campaign was a long one – extra blankets, greatcoat, and meal sacks with extra rations would all be attached, as well as clothing and additional pistols and ammunition. Generally, troopers tried not to overload their horses, and in hot climates, short pursuits could be undertaken with only the saddle, canteen and some forage and rations carried. This reduced both men and animals to a pitiful state when food and water ran out. Cavalry mounts were selectd from stockbreeders for their size (14–16 hands on average) and temperament, although in practice many fell below this ideal. They suffered badly on campaign with anything up to 75 per cent being rendered 'unfit for service'.

E2: Model 1874 McClellan saddle

Originally designed by Captain George McClellan, 1st Cavalry in 1855, the McClellan became the standard pattern saddle used throughout the Indian wars. The pattern illustrated has the carbine socket and skirts in place, and is in black leather, but saddles could also be found in varying shades of brown and, on campaign, the skirts would often be removed. Extra blankets and a poncho would be put underneath to protect the horse's back and a blanket may also be laid on top of the saddle itself to help cushion

An atmospheric photo of a sergeant walking his horse, whilst on campaign in the South-west, circa 1893. He has the 1885 drab campaign hat, 1883 sack coat and 1885 Mills belt. His one-pint tin mug is clearly visible strapped to the saddlebag. (Arizona Historical Society Wister Collection)

the trooper's behind. The rawhide that covered the McClellan was glued and stitched on to the wooden frame of the saddle, but once soaked and sun-dried a few times on campaign, it soon split, quickly rendering the whole saddle useless. Generally, two years of service was the maximum a McClellan could absorb before needing replacement.

F1: Sergeant, US Cavalry, 1876

This is the regulation issue uniform rarely seen on campaign. He wears the floppy-brimmed 1872 campaign hat, and blouse of 1874 pattern, with branch-of-service piping. His trousers are 1872 issue, with two top-opening pockets, (covered by the blouse); they have been reinforced with canvas at the seat. His carbine sling, sabre belt, holster and sabre are all of Civil War pattern, although the cap pouch visible next to the sword hilt is now used for revolver ammunition. Boots and brass spurs are regulation issue. His carbine is an 1873 Springfield.

This uniform was hot in summer and cold in winter, and had a tendency to rapidly fall apart. Few troopers who started a campaign dressed like this would finish it looking the same.

F2: 1872 forage cap

An improved version of the civil war 'bummer', the 1872 pattern was a more shaped fit, utilising less material in the body, and giving it a less floppy appearance. It was inspired by the French 'Kepi', but was not nearly as smart, and caused no end of problems when worn on campaign. It absorbed water, and provided no protection for the nape of the neck in hot weather. The leather peak would sag and unless a very good fit, the jogging motion of riding would cause the crown to bounce up and down. 'An useless rag' was one of the more printable descriptions of it.

F3: 1855 Hardee hat

A stiff, black, felt hat that pre-dated the Civil War, it was not seen in frontier campaigns in its illustrated form, which depicts an officer's pattern with gilded wire insignia. When on campaign, the feather was usually removed, the flapped brim dropped down, and the crown pummelled into a more comfortable shape. All wool-felt hats suffered badly in the rain, and the Hardee, like the trooper's wide-brimmed hat, would have sagged badly when wet. It was not used beyond about 1870, most troopers preferring civilian made items.

F4: 1875 campaign hat

An attempt by the Army to produce a serviceable hat after the badly designed, wide-brimmed, 1872 slouch hat. It was of wool-felt construction with leather sweat band and was based on the popular East Coast, broad-brimmed slouch hat. It had a small vent-hole each side of the crown, and was a creditable attempt at solving the problem of functional headgear. Soldiers, however, still preferred to purchase civilian hats, and the 1875 never became popular.

G: Cleaning and repairs

NCOs cleaning up after a campaign, c.1879. These men are wearing a practical mixture of regulation and non-regulation clothing, indeed only the yellow rank-stripes on their trousers indicate they are actually soldiers. Campaign life could be very tough on animals and weapons, and cleaning up was always a priority on return from campaign. The horse was every trooper's first concern. Each man was responsible for the maintenance of his mount and equipment, and penalties could be severe if he failed to take good care of them. The man at the left tends to the grooming of his horse, prior to his personal grooming, which will involve a visit to the post's barber for a haircut. Rifles and pistols suffered badly in the Midwest through the effects of rain, grit and sun, and if any action had been seen the black powder residue in the firearms would quickly turn into a corrosive acid. Rudimentary cleaning kits were carried, but time did not always permit proper care to be taken of firearms or swords. Carbines with broken stocks, revolvers with broken main-springs or jammed cylinders could not be repaired in the field, and would be exchanged on return to camp for serviceable weapons. Most major posts had an armourer, blacksmith and harness-maker to repair or refurbish damaged equipment and weapons. What could not be repaired was returned to depot for exchange. Sabres rusted very quickly, and it was nearly impossible to keep them clean in the field. The NCO illustrated here is using an oily rag to burnish the blade. If rust was very bad the post armourer would file it off, and re-polish the blade as best as he could. Old shirts and blankets were highly valued as cleaning rags, as the Army did not provide such necessities. Officers had the luxury of a groom who would take care of their horses, and a personal servant who was responsible for his uniform and equipment.

H: Crook on campaign against the Apaches, Arizona c.1873

Of all the South-western tribes, the Apaches were probably the most cunning, cruel and hardy. Gen. Crook was not a man to underestimate his enemy, and he made full use of the adage, 'It takes an Apache to catch an Apache'. Using trusted native scouts, his cavalry were able to track their enemy into the inhospitable deserts of Texas, New Mexico and Arizona. White Army scouts were also a valuable asset, once they had learned the Apache ways of fighting and how to best survive in the pitiless heat. Many adopted Indian ways of dress, as illustrated here, with high leg moccasin boots, to protect against plants like the Spanish Bayonet, whose razor-edged, spiked leaves could cut to the bone. Ambush was the most common form of attack, and troopers had to be on their guard. Gen. Crook habitually carried a short-barrelled shotgun (deadly at close range) and the Cavalry scout wears his revolver in a civilian-type open-topped holster, making the pistol more accessible in a hurry.

The Apache scout is examining a trail for signs of activity. Good scouts could track horses across rock by detecting signs that would be invisible to a white man. Most native scouts were armed with the latest weapons, and this man has the Springfield rifle as issued to the infantry. Wherever possible, they would equip themselves with captured or purchased firearms, and it was not uncommon for scouts to be armed with more modern weapons than regular troopers.

The harshness of the climate exacted a terrible price from both men and animals, and horses could collapse after a week on patrol. Crook always favoured the mule, more sure-footed than a horse and generally hardier. Apache warriors would use horses until they dropped, then switch to another, often eating the first animal after it expired. Although eventually won over by promises of food and reservation lands, the Apache were never truly subdued, despite being constantly outnumbered. US troopers were impressed at the Apache's ability to survive in a land that conspired against all forms of life.

I: Sabre practice, 1874

Training for recruits was rudimentary at best, and proper facilities for initiating troopers into Cavalry life were not provided until the 1880s. Many post commanders were concerned at this lack of instruction and took it upon themselves to ensure men were given at least basic training. In this illustration, a trooper is practicing sabre drill, a notoriously difficult skill to master.

The sabre was designed for both piercing and slashing, and it required considerable dexterity to control a galloping horse and wield a sword at the same time. In theory, a charging cavalryman should hold the sabre straight out in front of him, with his wrist twisted round to the right. This ensured the curved, sharp edge of the sabre was uppermost with the point angled down, so that when striking an enemy the weight of the blow forced the blade up and out of the body, preventing it becoming stuck, and being dragged from the trooper's grasp as the victim fell. In practice, this rarely happened, as excited soldiers slashed at any brave who came near, usually with little effect. In practical terms, the sabre was of little use in plains warfare, particularly as the Indians made increasingly effective use of firearms. Although they felt great affection for the sabre, few troopers had cause to use it in anger, but it remained in service as a symbol.

J: Mounted action, c.1874

The US Cavalry seldom excelled in open warfare with Indians, being unable to match them in endurance, stealth and cunning. Most 'victories' were against encamped Indian bands as illustrated here. This reconstruction shows well the variety of uniforms and weapons that could be found in a troop. The man in the foreground is using a .45 Colt and carrying a newly-issued 1873 Springfield carbine, whilst the man on the right shoots a .50/70 Sharps — affectionately known as 'Ole Reliable'.

Indians caught by surprise were seldom able to reply with the same volume of firepower; generally they were more concerned with ensuring their women and children were moved to safety. As a result, casualties were often heavy, with few losses to the troopers.

Material losses, particularly in winter, were often more serious to the Indians, as their food, clothing and ponies were captured or destroyed. There was little braves could do in the face of a Cavalry charge, particularly if the Cavalry commander was shrewd

2 pdr. Hotchkiss gun used at Wounded Knee. The soldier kneeling to the left wears a muskrat cap and webbing belt with the brass 'US' buckle, first adopted in 1872. (Library of Congress)

enough to deploy his men in two 'pincer' columns. For the cavalrymen, the thrill of a charge compensated for the frustrating hours of chasing an invisible foe. Accusations of unnecessary brutality were often levelled at the troopers, but in the dust, confusion and excitement, it was difficult to keep a clear head. Sometimes unplanned acts of heroism occurred. On one occasion a trooper's horse bolted during an attack on a Sioux encampment, carrying the terrified man right through the village. On reaching the safety of the other side, the trooper reloaded his revolver with shaking hands, at which point his horse, presumably missing the company of the other troop mounts, promptly bolted back again. The bewildered trooper was subsequently awarded the Medal of Honor for gallentry. Others weren't so fortunate, and any man unhorsed in an attack was doomed, for there was rarely time for a bunky to go back for him. Such attacks whilst glorious, were infrequent and ineffectual, but did serve to show the Indians that

nowhere was safe, particularly in winter. Wherever they went, the US Cavalry followed.

K: Dismounted action, c.1885

A skirmish in the South-west. The troopers have dismounted to take up defensive positions as laid down in the Army manual. Working in groups of four, one man was detailed to hold the reins of the horses, whilst the other three fought on foot, working forward with the other men of the company in an effort to push the hostiles back. This was a good tactic in theory, but against Indians, theory usually broke down. The Indians rapidly realised that without their mounts, cavalrymen were no match for them, so they attempted to scatter the horses, and the soldier guarding them was the primary target. Many braves carried bone whistles which gave out a piercing shriek often causing the animals to bolt. Such tactics were used very successfully on Maj. Reno's command at the Little Big Horn.

Two of the troopers illustrated have abandoned their jammed Springfield carbines and are using their .45 Colt revolvers, but once these were empty, the soldiers would be virtually defenceless until they could reload. Cavalrymen reduced to fighting on foot were rarely able to defeat Indians, a fact of which both sides were only too aware.

L1: Corporal, US Cavalry, cold weather clothing, 1880

Troopers feared the cold much more than the heat, which they accepted as normal for the West. As with most issued equipment, the clothing supplied was inadequate to cope with the cold. The caped overcoat illustrated was neither wind nor waterproof, and even when worn with a rubber poncho was insufficient for winter temperatures that chilled a cup of coffee as soon as it was poured from the pot. Gauntlets were worn most of the time, to keep the hands warm, and to stop the reins chafing. In very cold conditions, fur overmitts would be worn, and the coat stuffed with straw or dried grass to provide an insulating layer. The rubber and canvas boots were an improvement on the issue boot, but were cumbersome and impractical for riding. Warm headgear was always a problem. Slouch hats stuffed with straw then tied on the head with a wool scarf provided a partial solution, but were hardly ideal. A fur hat, such as the Buffalo skin example shown here, was by far the best solution, when such an item could be obtained.

L2: Buffalo skin coat

Indians particularly relied upon the buffalo for clothing in winter, and US troopers rapidly copied this practice. The coat illustrated has a quilt cotton lining and would most likely be owned by an officer, although many troopers purchased them. Some were brought with company funds and were handed out to men on guard duty, each sentry passing the coat onto the next. Freezing to death on guard was common, and such coats were vital for survival.

L3: Buffalo skin hat

Hats of this pattern were worn throughout the Indian Wars. Some, like the one illustrated, were of buffalo, others were made of seal, muskrat or beaver. The hat could be folded down to provide good protection for the ears and neck, but a good thick scarf would still be needed, as the nose was particularly susceptible to frostbite. It was one of the few items of headgear that was popular with the troopers.

A fatigue party of troopers at Fort Grant, Arizona, circa 1880. The only clue to their military background is the guard on the right. (Arizona Historical Society)

L4: 1873 canvas and buffalo skin overshoe
Although clumsy the overshoes were partly successful as they provided much needed insulation for the feet. Few cavalrymen survived a winter campaign in ordinary boots alone without the loss of a few toes, for the feet were notoriously difficult to protect. Thick felt overboots, stuffed with straw worked quite well if a soldier was on sentry duty; and a later pattern rubber 'Arctic overshoe' went some way towards providing full waterproofing. However, no suitable compromise was ever reached that enabled the trooper to ride and keep his feet warm. As a result cavalrymen adopted a wide range of civilian footwear.

Bibliography
Barnitz, Albert & Jenny. *Life in Custer's Cavalry*, Ed. R.M. Utley (Lincoln, Nebraska 1988)
Betinez, Jason, with W.S. Nye. *I fought with Geronimo* (Harrisburg, Pennsylvania 1959)
Bourke, John G. *An Apache Campaign in the Sierra Madre* (New York 1958)
Brown, Dee. *The Fetterman Massacre* (Lincoln, Nebraska 1972)
Brown, Dee. *Bury My Heart at Wounded Knee* (London 1972)
Carrington, Frances C. *Army Life on the Plains* (New York 1971)
du Mont, John S. *Custer Battleguns* (Canaan, New Hampshire 1988)
Hutchins, James S. *Boots & Saddles at the Little Bighorn* (Ft. Collins, Colorado 1976)
Katcher, Philip. *US Cavalry on the Plains, 1850–90* (London 1985)
Katcher, Philip. *The American Indian Wars, 1860–90* (London 1977)
King, Capt. Charles. *Campaigning with Crook* (Norman, Oklahoma 1989)
Marquis, Thomas B. *Keep the last bullet for yourself* (Algonac, Michigan 1987)
Marshall, S.L.A. *Crimsoned Prairie* (New York 1972)
Mulford, Ami F. *Fighting Indians in the 7th U.S. Cavalry* (New York 1899)
Reedstrom, Ernest L. *Bugles, Banners and War Bonnets* (Caldwell Idaho 1977)
Rickey, Don. *Forty Miles a day on Beans and Hay* (Norman, Oklahoma 1989)
Spotts, David L. *Campaigning with Custer* (Lincoln, Nebraska 1988)
Steffan, Randy. *The Horse Soldiers, Vol II, 1851–1880* (Norman, Oklahoma 1987)
Stewart, Edgar. *Custer's Luck* (Norman, Oklahoma 1987)
Time-Life Books. Ed. Constable, George. *The Soldiers* (New York 1972)
Urwin, Gregory J. *The United States Cavalry* (New York 1985)
Utley, R.M., and Washburn, W.E. *Indian Wars* (New York 1985)
Utley, R.M. *Bluecoats and Redskins* (London 1973)

GLOSSARY

Black Powder A mix of 15 per cent charcoal, 10 per cent sulphur and 75 per cent potassium nitrate. A propellant used for all cartridges up until about 1890.
Bowie A large fighting knife whose invention was incorrectly accredited to Col. J. Bowie. It has a single-edged blade, with curved false edge. Many were very large, measuring a foot in length.
Buckskin A strong soft thick leather made from deer or goatskin. Usually yellow or fawn in colour.
Bummer The Civil War kepi, made of blue wool with a leather peak, it was generally regarded as useless as headwear.
Bunky A bunkmate, or good friend.

Col. Miles (centre), staff and troopers brave a Montana winter prior to attacking the Sioux in 1877. They wear an assortment of privately purchased fur coats. The officer at the left also has matching knee boots. (National Archives)

Calibre The internal dimension of a barrel.

Cantle The raised rear portion of a saddle.

Carbine A rifle of reduced barrel length, usually firing a reduced power cartridge.

Centrefire A cartridge with a primer mounted centrally in its base. Of greater strength than the rimfire. It could be easily reloaded once fired. In general use from about 1872.

Cholera An intestinal disease caused by impure water. Usually fatal.

Colt A company formed by Samuel Colt (1814–1862) who pioneered mass production and parts interchangeability. The revolver design, although not invented by Colt, was effective enough to gain military interest, and from 1847, the factory was engaged in producing a wide range of pistols.

Double-action A firearm that can be fired by squeezing the trigger, without first manually cocking the hammer.

Ejector A spring-loaded rod which enabled fired cases to be removed from the cylinder of a revolver.

Entry and Exit Wounds A self-explanatory term; the exit wound of a bullet is usually two to four times greater in size than the entry wound.

Fatigues Either a general term relating to work undertaken, e.g. cookhouse fatigues, or a specific term applied to the loose white jacket and trousers issued to prevent soiling of the service uniform.

Gate-loading Single-action revolvers (e.g. Colt .45) had fixed cylinders. Cartridges had to be loaded one at a time through an aperture (gate) at the rear.

Garry Owen A popular Irish tune adopted as the marching song of the 7th Cavalry.

Gatling Gun The invention of Dr. R. Gatling (1818–1903). It had six rotating barrels, but was cumbersome and heavy being mounted on an artillery carriage.

Gun Powder see **Black Powder**.

Hash A meal consisting of fried meat, mixed with anything else that was available – crushed biscuit, vegetables or bacon fat.

Hotchkiss A small quick-firing, 2 pdr. cannon which used high explosive or case shot. Often used with great effect in remote areas inaccessible to artillery.

Jerky Dried beef. It looked and tasted like boot leather but was nutritious and often all that was available.

Kepi A peaked cap based on the French military pattern.

Kersey A coarse woollen cloth, not renowned for its longevity.

Lariat A length of rope carried on the saddle.

Lever-action Rifles such as Winchesters, which could be cocked by use of a hand lever forming part of the trigger guard.

Magazine A tube containing cartridges one of which

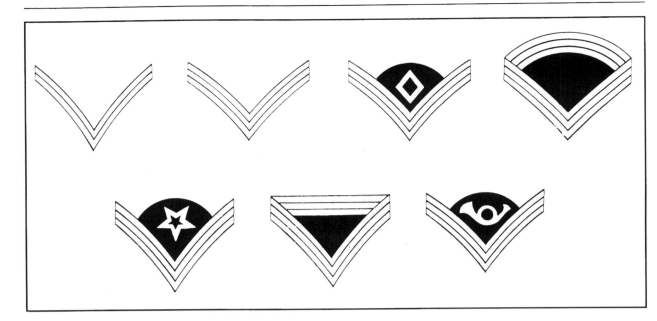

would be loaded into the breech upon cocking.

Mills Belt A woven cotton belt of the type normally now referred to as webbing. Reputed to have been invented by Capt. Anson Mills, US Cavalry.

Mutilation A practice favoured by Indians, which involved removal of limbs and organs, or deeply slashing the corpse with knives or tomahawks. It was done to prevent the spirit of the dead ascending to the afterlife. Troopers found the practice abhorrent.

Muzzle The forward end of a barrel.

Percussion A form of ignition relying on the hammer striking a copper cap filled with fulminate.

Pommel The raised 'horn' at the front of a saddle, providing an anchor point for a rope, resting place for a carbine and hand grip in rough terrain.

Poncho A rubberised cape, designed to be worn mounted or on foot. Two could be joined together to form a small tent.

Rawhide Natural, untreated cow leather.

Remington Founded in Ilion, New York, by Eliphalet Remington in 1816, the company made a large number of solidly contructed firearms, including the .44 Army revolver and Rolling Block rifle.

Rimfire A cartridge detonated by the firing pin striking the edge of the case, which contains a fulminate priming compound. Rimfires were structurally weak, and could not be reloaded once fired.

Sabre Specifically a curve-bladed Cavalry weapon, designed for slashing.

Sack Coat The four- or five-button service tunic. So called because of its fit.

Scurvy Vitamin deficiency – it resulted in loss of teeth and hair and bleeding gums. In extreme cases it could be fatal.

Shaman An Indian holy man regarded by many as a prophet. Often held more authority than tribal chiefs.

Sharps A breech-loading percussion rifle patented by Christian Sharps (1811–1874) in 1848. After the Civil War, hundreds of the rifles were produced using centre-fire cartridges and were used in great numbers for buffalo hunting.

Single-action A firearm that requires the hammer to be manually cocked before each shot.

Sling A wide, leather shoulder belt with a snap-hook designed to carry the carbine whilst on horseback.

Smith & Wesson Formed by Horace Smith (1808–1893) and Daniel B. Wesson (1825–1906) the company began making hinged-frame revolvers which evolved into the self-ejecting models of 1869. Arguably better designed than the Colts, the company were a major supplier of pistols.

Snowbird Army slang for a deserter.

Spencer A magazine-fed, rimfire rifle patented by Christopher Spencer (1833–1922) in 1860. It was the first metallic-cartridge, repeating firearm used in warfare.

Stable-frock A white, loose-fitting jacket worn to protect the uniform during fatigues.

Surcingle A wide, woven strap that covers both saddle and girth on a horse for added security.

Sword knot A leather wrist-strap to prevent the trooper dropping the sword if he loosens his grip.

Top-break The system of unlocking a revolver to extract the cartridges. A latch forward of the hammer would be lifted, allowing the hinged barrel and cylinder to drop forward and down.

Verdigris A green mould that always appears on copper or brass that is in contact with leather.

Winchester The company founded by Oliver Winchester (1810–1880) based on the Volcanic Arms Company, who produced an early lever-action repeating pistol. His Henry repeating rifle (1860) was used in limited numbers during the Civil War, and the improved Winchester model became one of the most popular rifles in the West.

INDEX

(References to illustrations are shown in **bold**. Plates are shown with page and caption locators in brackets.)